YALE STUDIES IN RELIGIOUS EDUCATION
XVIII

RELIGION IN HIGHER EDUCATION AMONG NEGROES

RELIGION
IN HIGHER EDUCATION
AMONG NEGROES

BY

RICHARD I. McKINNEY

President, Storer College
Harpers Ferry, West Virginia

NEW HAVEN · YALE UNIVERSITY PRESS

LONDON · HUMPHREY MILFORD · OXFORD UNIVERSITY PRESS

1945

TO

MY MOTHER

AND

THE MEMORY OF MY FATHER

PREFACE

THIS study would not have come to its present stage without the active interest of many individuals too numerous to mention in detail. The investigation owes its impetus to the grant of a fellowship by the National Council on Religion in Higher Education, to which, and especially to its former Executive Director, Miss Martha H. Biehle, the writer owes immeasurable thanks for counsel and assistance. Without the material encouragement also of the Edward W. Hazen Foundation the investigation would hardly have been completed. Acknowledgments are due, in addition, to the faculty of the Andover Newton Theological School for material assistance through a study grant on the Turner Fellowship.

For the technical phases of the study the writer is indebted to his advisers on the faculty of Yale University. To Dr. Clarence P. Shedd are due thanks for counsel and direction in the general as well as the specific problem area; to Dr. Hugh Hartshorne, Research Associate in Religion, and to Dean Luther A. Weigle of the Yale Divinity School acknowledgments are hereby extended for many helpful suggestions and for guidance in the carrying forward of the study.

The writer is also indebted to a committee of college administrators appointed from its membership by the National Council on Religion in Higher Education for assistance in the execution of the field-study phases of the investigation. This committee consisted of President Benjamin E. Mays of Morehouse College, Chairman, President Thomas E. Jones of Fisk University, and Dean W. Stuart Nelson of the School of Religion of Howard University. Later augmented by President Mordecai W. Johnson of Howard University, this committee, upon the completion of the study, kindly undertook to solicit funds from the colleges for Negroes to assist in the publication of this book. Thanks are due not only to these men but to the many other college presidents, teachers, and students who in various ways contributed to the assembling of the material of this study and to its publication.

President-emeritus William J. Clark and President John M. Ellison of Virginia Union University kindly extended the writer leaves of absence and otherwise rendered valuable help. Dr. Ambrose Caliver, Senior Specialist in Negro Education in the United States Office of Education, has given generously of his time and encouragement. To Dr. Howard Thurman, Dean of the Chapel of Howard University, the writer owes a debt of gratitude for the stimulus of interest in and enthusiasm for the possibilities of religion in higher education. For gracious assistance in typing the original manuscript thanks are due to Mrs. Ann Florant.

Finally, to his wife the writer acknowledges obligations which are much more profoundly felt than adequately described.

R. I. M.

Harpers Ferry, West Virginia
  May 15, 1945

ACKNOWLEDGMENTS

I wish to thank the following publishers for their kind permission to quote the copyrighted publications as listed: D. Appleton-Century Company, E. A. Fitzpatrick, *Readings in the Philosophy of Education;* The Association Press, Clarence P. Shedd, *Two Centuries of Student Christian Movements;* Bureau of Publications, Teachers College, Columbia University, D. O. W. Holmes, *The Evolution of the Negro College; Christian Education,* XX and XXI, No. 1; Columbia University Press, B. G. Gallagher, *American Caste and the Negro College; The Crisis,* XLVIII; The Epworth Press, Nehemiah Curnock, ed., *The Journal of John Wesley;* Harper & Brothers, Richard Wright, *Native Son;* Houghton Mifflin Company, Franklin Bobbitt, *The Curriculum,* and *The Journal of John Woolman; The Journal of Negro Education,* IX; G. P. Putnam's Sons, George L. Clark, *A History of Connecticut,* and Carter G. Woodson, *The Education of the Negro Prior to 1861; The Sunday School Informer,* V; University of Pennsylvania Press, *Religion and the Modern World;* The Viking Press, James Weldon Johnson, *Along This Way.*

Thanks are due also to the following authors for permission to quote from their unpublished monographs: Byron K. Armstrong, "Factors in the Formulation of a Collegiate Program for Negroes"; Ellis O. Knox, "The Trend of Progress in the Light of New Educational Concepts in a Group of American Colleges Dominated by Religious Influences."

R. I. M.

INTRODUCTION

THAT religion has always played a dynamic role in the founding and maintenance of American colleges has been a long-recognized fact. As Tewksbury's [1] definitive study shows, the forces and ideals of religion were dominant factors in the establishment of the American colleges before the Civil War. Moreover, studies by Shedd show not only that organized religion has continued to exert interest in youth as they go to public institutions but also that students themselves, through almost the entire history of American higher education, have tended to organize and maintain voluntary religious organizations. [2]

But it is more strikingly true of Negro education than of any other educational tradition that religious interests and forces have been the primary determining factors in the rise and perpetuation of higher institutions of learning. As Holmes well says, the Negro college is largely the product of the missionary enterprise. [3] With two or three exceptions, the present institutions of higher learning for Negroes in America were established after the Civil War. Pioneering in this undertaking were men and women representing various religious organizations who sought to lay the foundations for the education of the Negro which would embody definitely religious principles.

The problem for investigation lies in the area of higher education among a specific sociological group, the Negro people. It also lies within the area of the larger problem, independent of racial considerations, of the place of religion in higher education. Some studies have been made with reference to the development and function of higher education among Negroes, and recently the United States Office of Education completed a comprehensive survey of the status of higher education among this group. To date, however, no comprehensive study has been made which has attempted to show the role which religion is now playing in the policies and programs of the Negro college. Such a study requires a consideration of the background of Negro life in this country and

1. Donald Tewksbury, *The Founding of the American Colleges and Universities Before the Civil War* (New York, Bureau of Publications, Teachers College, Columbia University, 1932), pp. 55 ff.

2. C. P. Shedd, *The Church Follows Its Students* (New Haven, Yale University Press, 1938). C. P. Shedd, *Two Centuries of Student Christian Movements* (New York, Association Press, 1934).

3. D. O. W. Holmes, *The Evolution of the Negro College* (New York, Bureau of Publications, Teachers College, Columbia University, 1934), p. vi.

of the way in which religious organizations and foundations have attempted to enhance the educational and cultural status of this minority group by establishing and perpetuating schools of learning. More specifically, it necessitates a consideration of the objectives of Negro higher education in terms of the personality of the individual and the bearing of his environment upon it, as well as some understanding of how religion may function in determining the kind of personality the colleges produce.

To some observers it has seemed that the colleges for Negroes have moved away, or are beginning to move away, from many of the emphases of traditional religion. It is apparent that the development of scientific research has influenced the religious outlook of the Negro intelligentsia, and that a reëvaluation of religion and of its place in the life of the group is being made. A new conception of the relation of religion to the social system of which the Negro is a part is observable among certain Negro leaders. In addition to this, the secularism characteristic of the present age inevitably influences all sociological groups regardless of race.

Stated in a simple hypothesis, then, our problem is embodied in the following proposition: The religious policies, objectives, curricula, programs, and activities of the colleges for Negroes, vitally affected by current intellectual and social trends, are of strategic importance in the realization of the total and ultimate objectives of these institutions, so that an understanding of the present significance and function of religion in higher education among Negroes must be had.

In the light of the foregoing statement of the nature of the study, the purpose of this investigation is to determine the present status of the religious policies and programs in the colleges for Negroes and to examine the significance of these for the Negro student in view of the social setting of the education of this minority group.

Administrators and faculties of colleges are becoming increasingly interested in the problem of the function of religion in the realization of their ultimate objectives. In issuing a call to the presidents of Negro colleges to participate in a faculty conference held in February, 1940, on the theme "Religion and the College for Negroes," ten presidents of Negro colleges subscribed to the following statement:

There never was a time in our national life when it is more necessary than now to face quite realistically the challenge of religion to our youth. There are many who are of the opinion that our colleges tend to deaden rather than quicken the interest of students in the great timeless issues of religion. They place the responsibility for this upon the age in which we live; the loss of the service motive in our institutions; the attitude of indifference or hostility toward religion on the part of college faculties. . . . Obviously there is confusion as to the actual state of religion on our campuses today. . . .[4]

Added significance is attached to the present study because of the general interest in the place of religion in higher education that is observable at the present time. It is noteworthy that in recently celebrating its tricentennial the University of Pennsylvania sponsored a symposium on the theme, "Religion in the Modern World." Speaking at this celebration, Dr. Robert L. Calhoun of Yale University said,

High religion, in short, and intellectual enterprise belong together. Each gains from close association with the other. The two in conjunction, but neither one by itself, can move with hope toward more effective conquest of the chaos that again and again threatens to engulf human living. That way lies whatever chance we may have for a more humane world.[5]

It is the hope that the present study of the status of religion in the colleges for Negroes will be useful in determining along what lines these institutions may move in the future planning of their religious objectives, policies, and programs.

The sources of the study are the general investigations of religion in higher education as well as the specific studies of the social system in which Negro education proceeds. Recourse has been had also to studies in the development of the Negro college. In addition to these, data from both college officials and students have been secured from a selected group of Negro institutions.

The study comprises four general procedures. First, instruments of investigation were designed to exhibit data on the present administrative provisions for religious work on the campus such as religious exercises, directors of religious life, courses and teachers in the field of religion, budgetary provisions for religion, voluntary student religious organizations, and the attitudes of students toward the religious life and program of the college. After these instruments were prepared and checked with a small experimental group, the final forms were drawn up for use in the entire study.

Secondly, that the study might have validity for a particular group of colleges, it was thought best to select for more intensive study a group of Class *A* Negro institutions representing church-related, private, and public types of control. Sixteen such schools were selected, divided al-

4. Quoted from the letter sent to 80 presidents of Negro institutions. The conference was sponsored by the Fellowship of Religious Workers in Colleges for Negroes.

5. Jacques Maritain *et al.*, *Religion and the Modern World* (Philadelphia, University of Pennsylvania Press, 1941), p. 71.

most equally among these three types and representing proportionate demoninational as well as geographical distribution. The investigator personally visited these schools for first-hand observations and on the campus of each one remained from two and a half to four days. During this time consultations were held with the college administrators and with representative faculty people both individually and in groups; meanwhile questionnaires pertaining to the administrative provisions for religion were filled out. In addition to this, conferences and interviews were held with student leaders. Opportunities were given by college authorities to visit classes of junior and senior classification in which the investigator personally administered questionnaires dealing with the attitudes of upperclassmen toward the religious life of the campus. Attempts were made to find those classes which represented a cross section of academic interests among the students.

Thirdly, copies of each type of questionnaire were mailed to a number of other institutions where college officials coöperated in having them properly executed. In addition to the sixteen colleges which the investigator personally visited, therefore, complete or partial information was obtained from 34 other institutions. All of these statistics are representative primarily of the total picture in the Class A institutions. But it is felt that they are also suggestive for all four-year Negro colleges. Approximately 47 per cent of the colleges from which data are available were Class A institutions.

Finally, when the questionnaires were all returned, those pertaining to administrative religious provisions and student organizations were then analyzed by the investigator. The questionnaires filled out by upperclassmen, 1,345 in all, were coded and then analyzed by the mechanical process used in business-machine computations. Upon the completion of the tabulation of the questionnaires, the results of these, as well as of the less objective phases of the study such as personal interviews and group consultations, were interpreted.[6]

6. The complete results of this study were presented as a dissertation in candidacy for the degree of Doctor of Philosophy in Yale University and are on file in the Sterling Memorial Library.

CONTENTS

LIST OF TABLES

RELIGION IN HIGHER EDUCATION
AMONG NEGROES

I

RELIGION AND THE RISE OF HIGHER EDUCATION
AMONG NEGROES IN THE UNITED STATES

THE present situation of religion in Negro colleges can best be understood by seeing in historical perspective the development of Negro life and schools in this country.[1] This development, which began to take an entirely new form about eighty years ago, is character-

1. Some of the material for this background chapter has been taken from the original sources themselves, but most of it has come from the significant secondary works that are available in the field of Negro history and education. From a survey of the literature it is seen that, on the historical side, studies made by Woodson, Brawley, and Johnson are of the first rank (C. G. Woodson, *The Negro in Our History* [Washington, Associated Publishers, 1931]; Benjamin Brawley, *A Social History of the American Negro* [New York, Macmillan Co., 1921]; C. S. Johnson, *The Negro in American Civilization* [New York, Henry Holt & Co., 1930].) With respect to the development and present status of Negro education itself, such studies as those made by Bond, Holmes, Woodson and Gallagher have been definitive (H. M. Bond, *The Education of the Negro in the American Social Order* [New York, Prentice-Hall Co., 1934]; D. O. W. Holmes, *The Evolution of the Negro College* [New York, Bureau of Publications, Teachers College, Columbia University, 1934]; C. G. Woodson, *The Education of the Negro Prior to 1861* [New York, G. P. Putnam's Sons, 1915]; B. G. Gallagher, *American Caste and the Negro College* [New York, Columbia University Press, 1938].) In addition to the above studies, the United States Office of Education has made three comprehensive surveys of higher education among Negroes. The first of these paved the way for the standardization movement in Negro schools (T. J. Jones, *Negro Education, A Study of the Private and Higher Schools for Colored People in the United States* [Washington, United States Government Printing Office, 1916, 2 vols.] and the second, ten years later, gave notable impetus to the improvement of the quality of education Negroes received on the college level (A. J. Klein, *Survey of Negro Colleges and Universities*, United States Bureau of Education Bulletin, 1926, No. 7 [Washington, United States Government Printing Office, 1928].) The publication of the third study was not completed at the time of this investigation.

Daniel's study of *The Education of Negro Ministers* (New York, George H. Doran Co., 1925) is the only book published to date specifically in its field, but, since that volume is primarily concerned with theological education, it does not have the scope that is needed for a thorough-going study of religion in higher education among Negroes. A recent doctoral dissertation, yet unpublished (Henry M. Johnson, "The Methodist Episcopal Church and the Education of Southern Negroes [1862–1900]" [Yale University, New Haven, 1939]), as well as Holmes' study referred to above, have made a significant beginning in the matter of tracing comprehensively the place of religion in the rise of Negro education.

ized by wistful hopes, courageous sacrifices, some ennobling successes, and some disappointing failures. But actually, as we shall see, we must go back further than the Civil War to get a clear picture of what has been the relation of religion to Negro education.

The historical relation of religion to higher education in America. The problem of the place of religion in higher education among Negroes is not conceived here to be entirely separate from the issues of religion in higher education generally. In so far as the peculiar social and psychological setting in which the education of this minority group is carried on is fundamentally different, to that extent does the problem with which we are concerned assume characteristics not to be found in the educational situation among the more privileged groups. Since the practices of the majority often have been and still are the standards of the minority as far as the dependence of Negro education upon the example of white colleges is concerned, it is desirable, if for no other reason, to see how the relation of religion to higher education has been historically conceived.

It is only in relatively recent years of educational history in America that there has been a problem associated with the relation of religion to higher education or to education as a whole. One of the most patent facts in the history of American colleges is their dependence historically upon religious forces and individuals for their origin. The people who founded the colleges had a very practical interest in religion, and it was taken for granted that religion should be one of the most important aspects of the life of the school.[2] Just as in the earliest history of education the custom was for the adult members of the group to teach the young all that the latter would need to make the best adjustment to society, including the rituals and ceremonials of religion as well as those arts of hunting and fighting by means of which survival was made possible,[3] the early settlers of this country felt it incumbent upon them to provide for the religious instruction of their youth in order that the kinds of ideals they cherished should not be lost. It is no accident, therefore, that the records of the founding of most of the American colleges prior to 1865 contain pointed references to the religious motives and ideals which were in the minds of the founders of these institutions. For them the relation of religion to education was dynamic and functional, so that the story of the rise of American higher education becomes a story of religious forces

2. Donald Tewksbury, *The Founding of the American Colleges and Universities Before the Civil War* (New York, Bureau of Publications, Teachers College, Columbia University, 1932), pp. 55 ff. C. F. Thwing, *A History of Higher Education in America* (New York, D. Appleton & Co., 1906), pp. 5, 6, 215 *et passim.* L. K. Patton, *The Purposes of the Church-Related Colleges* (New York, Bureau of Publications, Teachers College, Columbia University, 1940), p. 32.

3. W. H. Kilpatrick, *Education for a Changing Civilization* (New York, Macmillan Co., 1927), pp. 54–55.

seeking to make religion more effective in the lives of youth and in the life of society.

It is a striking fact that the dominating religious interest in the founding of the earliest colleges in this country parallels that in the establishment of the earliest Negro colleges. The emphasis in each case was upon the training of ministers and religious teachers. In each case this emphasis was gradually broadened in recognition of the need for a religiously educated laity as well as clergy. Educational institutions consequently came to be thought of as centers from which the leaven of the Christian religion might permeate the life of society. Of course, there were some other less idealistic motives behind the establishment of many of the denominational colleges. The desire of one religious sect to compete with another led to much waste of funds and energies. But, despite this fact, it can safely be said that the real fundamental motives in the founding of the schools was devotion to some spiritual ideal.

The secularization movement in American education was destined, however, to raise the issue of the unique place of religion in the schools. The rise of the state universities came in time seriously to challenge the supremacy of the denominational schools. As these schools were increasing, sectarianism was also increasing on a large scale. The injection of sectarianism into the schools prompted a controversy which eventually resulted in the almost complete secularization of American public education.[4] The rapid growth of public education on all levels was soon recognized as a fundamental factor sharpening the issue of the relation which religion ought to sustain to the educational process. Obviously, were it not for the fact that the nation was endeavoring to practice the principle of democracy in practically all aspects of its life there would have been no serious problem. The fundamental doctrine of religious liberty was highly cherished, along with a profound belief in the necessity of universal education to guarantee a stable democratic society. In establishing the ordinance for the government of the Northwest Territory in 1787, it was declared that "Religion, morality and knowledge being necessary to good government and happiness of mankind, schools and the means of education shall forever be encouraged." [5] For the next hundred years the development of the nation was along the lines of these principles.

The rapid growth of the publicly supported schools and colleges and the subsequent secularization of education posed a dilemma for American education which has not yet been satisfactorily solved. Believing in the principles of democracy and individual liberty, while at the same time

4. S. W. Brown, *The Secularization of American Education* (New York, Teachers College, Columbia University, 1912), chap. vi ff.

5. E. A. Fitzpatrick, ed., *Readings in the Philosophy of Education* (New York, D. Appleton-Century Co., 1936), p. 69.

believing in the value of religion for a sound society, the American people were faced with the problem of whether to inculcate and practice democracy in education at the expense of religious instruction or to insist on religious instruction in public education at the expense of certain democratic principles. Paradoxically, because they believed so much in their religious principles, the dilemma was solved by excluding religious teaching from the public schools. The secularization movement was therefore not a revolt against religion itself but against the dangers of sectarianism in public instruction. From this time on, as far as the public was concerned, the responsibility for systematic religious instruction became the responsibility of the church rather than of the school. Today it is clear that this attempt at solution has not proved entirely satisfactory, for it has resulted in leaving out of the public educational system that which many feel to be one of the most essential elements of man's life.

Negro education before the Civil War. The coming of the Negro to America began one year before the *Mayflower* touched Plymouth Rock. In 1619, at Jamestown, Virginia, the first group of Negroes were landed in this country, thus instituting a practice which was destined to have momentous consequences for the future of the nation. The next hundred years saw the slave trade developing slowly but by the time of the first American census in 1790 the Negro population had grown to 19.3 per cent of the total.[6] Because of the agricultural pursuits in which they were employed, it was natural that the great majority of the Negro population should have been in the southern part of colonial America, where today, in spite of large-scale migration during the last two decades, the majority of Negroes live.

During the colonial period as well as some three decades afterwards the majority attitude toward the education of Negroes was a favorable one. The more humanitarian slave owners realized that some minimum of education was essential in order to develop adequate communication and adaptation between master and slave. There were differences of opinion, however, with respect to just what kind of education Negroes should have.[7] Woodson has pointed out three different groups who favored the education of Negroes in this period. The first group comprised the slave owners who thought in terms of increased economic efficiency of their slaves. In various ways these masters gave their slaves opportunities for mental improvements; and when the opposition to the education of Negroes eventually developed the same owners often defied the laws and persisted in giving their slaves education. The second group favoring

6. Monroe N. Work, *Negro Year Book, 1925–26* (Tuskegee, Negro Year Book Publishing Co., 1925), p. 423.

7. C. G. Woodson, *The Education of the Negro Prior to 1861* (New York, G. P. Putnam's Sons, 1915), pp. 1–2.

education of Negroes were the humanitarians who, in sympathy with the downtrodden, felt that education was one means of improving their situation. Because the members of this group were for the most part neither slave owners nor inhabitants of the sections where the slaves lived, the practical application of their attitude could not be carried out effectively. The third group favoring the education of Negroes were those religious-minded people who, as Woodson says, "believing that the message of divine love came equally to all, taught slaves the English language that they might learn the principles of the Christian religion." [8] This third group was made up largely of missionaries, represented first of all by the Spanish and French Catholics, who went so far as to give free Negroes the best educational advantages obtainable. The work of the Catholics centered largely in Louisiana, and they made a significant contribution in agitating for more humane treatment of the slaves.[9]

One of the most enterprising organizations working to bring religious instruction to colonial America was the "Society for the Propagation of the Gospel to Foreign Parts." This organization was founded in 1701 by the English. The first president of this organization, "Thomas, Lord Bishop of Canterbury, Primate and Metropolitan of all England," was appointed by the King of England himself.[10] The primary purpose of this society was to bring religious instruction and privileges to all the colonists in North America; and, secondarily, its purpose was to bring the Gospel "to the Indians and Negroes." [11] One of the underlying purposes of this group was to counteract the influence which the Catholics were having among the Negroes. Eventually this came to be considered as the most important and significant part of the work of this society of the Church of England.

Other religious groups besides the European Catholics and the representatives of the Church of England sought to bring instruction to Negroes in the colonial era. In New England and in the Northern states several schools were begun for the education of Negroes,[12] while at the same time in most of the communities Negroes were allowed to attend the public schools along with whites.

What is said to be the first attempt to establish a mission exclusively for Negroes was the work of the Moravian or United Brothers who began a series of enterprises in the year 1738, the result of which, according to their reports, was the conversion of many enslaved and free Negroes to

8. *Ibid.*, p. 2.

9. M. A. Diggs, *Catholic Negro Education in the United States* (Washington, published by the author, 1936), chap. i.

10. C. C. Jones, *The Religious Instruction of Negroes in the United States* (Savannah, Thomas Purse, 1842), p. 4.

11. *Ibid.*

12. Woodson, *op. cit.*, p. 4.

the Christian faith and their regular instruction in Biblical principles.[13] This work was first established in Georgia and later spread to other states in the deep South.

In 1747 the Presbyterians in Virginia began an enterprise of providing regular religious instruction to Negroes which was continued over a long period of years. The leaders of this movement were the Reverend Samuel Davies and the Reverend John Todd of the Hanover Presbytery. While the work began in Hanover County, it was carried forward in as many as four other adjacent counties and in other parts of the South.[14] Davies wrote to John Wesley that about one half of the population of Virginia were Negroes, or around 150,000, and that, of those, around three hundred attended on his ministry. In commenting on the reaction of the slaves to the instruction he gave, Davies said,

A considerable number of them, about a hundred, have been baptised, after they had been fully instructed in the great truths of religion and had evidenced their sense of them by a life of strictest virtue. . . . There are multitudes of them in various parts who are eagerly desirous of instruction. They have generally little to read; and yet, to my agreeable surprise, sundry of them, by dint of application in their few leisure hours, have made such a progress that they are able to read their Bible, or a plain author, very intelligibly. But few of their masters will be at the expense of furnishing them with books. I have supplied them to the utmost of my ability.[15]

Methodist activity in the education of Negroes began with the interest and efforts of John Wesley himself. Wesley came to this country as a missionary to the Indians but he had a great concern for the welfare of Negroes. A study of his *Journal* reveals many references to his experiences and reflections concerning the capabilities of the Negro. The following item in his *Journal* indicates how Wesley thought the slaves might best be instructed: ". . . one of the easiest and shortest ways to instruct the American Negroes in Christianity would be, first, to inquire after and find out some of the most serious of the planters. Then, having inquired of them which of their slaves were best inclined and understood English, to go to them from plantation to plantation, staying as long as appeared necessary to each." [16] There is no indication in his *Journal* as to whether he ever made an attempt to carry out this plan.

That there was a great division of sentiment on the question of slavery and the welfare of the Negro among the Methodists is made clear by the separation of the Southern group from the Northern at the time when

13. C. C. Jones, *op. cit.*, p. 30.

14. *Ibid.*, p. 35.

15. Nehemiah Curnock, ed., *The Journal of the Rev. John Wesley, A.M.* (London, Epworth Press, 1938), IV, 125.

16. *Ibid.*, I, 353.

the slavery issue became the most crucial one in American life. Further mention of this will be made below.

Among the first of the religious groups to recognize and practice the principles of educational equality was the Society of Friends. Being for the most part humanitarian in their social outlook, they relatively early began to provide the opportunities for the education of Negroes, opportunities which were essentially equal to those of their own group. But this attitude of the Quakers was itself the result of a period of protest on the part of the Quaker leaders. When George Fox visited Barbados Island in 1671 he found that many Quakers there held slaves and he expressed his strong disapproval of the practice. Memorials against slavery were sent from time to time to various Quaker groups in America, but the first Quaker group to take an active stand against the practice was a group of German Friends who, in 1686, at Germantown, Pennsylvania, made a resolution against it. John Woolman, one of the most influential Quakers in the history of the group, was quite active in protesting against the evils of slavery and in seeking to foster the proper attitude among Friends for the welfare and instruction of Negroes. His labors and those of others were rewarded when the Yearly meeting in 1758 at Philadelphia, Pennsylvania, "agreed that the injunction of our Lord and Saviour to do to others as we would that others should do to us should induce Friends who held slaves to set them at liberty, making a Christian provision for them." [17]

In the schools which the Quakers established it appears that racial discrimination was not practiced. Writing of the schools of this period, Henry J. Cadbury says,

In early documents like Thomas Budd's *Good Order* the schools were to provide "that the children of the poor people, and the children of Indians may have like learning with the children of the rich people." While a hundred years later when freed Negroes became the special concern of the Society of Friends they bracketed together as beneficiaries of the local country meeting school funds children of poor Friends or of blacks, or as one Haddonfield testator puts it, "for schooling poor children of any color." [18]

With the coming of the social doctrines of "liberty, equality and fraternity" to American shores, the favorable attitude toward the education of Negroes increased. The result was a number of instances of the manumission of slaves. The consequent rise of schools for free Negroes and the rapid progress made by them under the new opportunities dispelled

17. John Woolman, *The Journal of John Woolman* (Whittier edition, Boston, Houghton Mifflin Co., 1871), p. 19.

18. *Two and a Half Centuries of Quaker Education,* Proceedings of the Anniversary Meeting held under the auspices of Friends' Council on Education, Tenth Month 20, 1931, Philadelphia, p. 12.

the doubt that Negroes were incapable of learning. To quote from Woodson on this point, "Negroes learned to appreciate and write poetry and contributed something to mathematics, science and philosophy. Furthermore . . . in conformity with the suggestion of Cotton Mather, Negroes were employed to teach white children." [19]

This growth of the intellectual and social development of the Negroes in America might have continued but for two or three conditions which arose and were destined to retard it considerably. In the North and East the economic and social status of the free Negroes began to cause some alarm to the white inhabitants of several communities. Many began to see Negroes primarily as an economic and moral liability in the community and made every effort to see that the number of Negroes in their towns did not increase too rapidly. A movement was begun in 1831 by free Negroes to establish a college for the young men of their group which would be devoted primarily to mechanical training. "The announcement of the plan met a storm of opposition; the city officials and the voters denounced it in a public meeting, did their best to defeat it, and their action was fatal to it." [20]

There is one very striking instance of the increasing misgiving on the part of some communities in the East as to the general effect of the presence and education of Negroes in their midst. A young Quaker lady, Miss Prudence Crandall, opened a school for girls at Canterbury, Connecticut, in 1831, a school which received at the outset the patronage of the most prominent families in the community. When the white patrons objected to the admittance of a colored girl to the school, Miss Crandall decided at length to change the school to one entirely for colored girls and accordingly dismissed the other students. In May, 1833, one month following the opening of the school to "young Ladies and little Misses of color," the residents of Canterbury were successful in getting the legislature of Connecticut to enact a law making the operation of such a school a criminal offense. Miss Crandall was adamant in her determination to operate this school despite the fact that she was duly arrested and convicted for breaking the new law. The circuit court sustained the judgment of the lower court, but this judgment was reversed by the Supreme Court of Errors in July, 1834.[21] Two months later a band of citizens stormed the school

19. Woodson, *op. cit.*, p. 6.

20. George L. Clark, *A History of Connecticut* (New York, G. P. Putnam's Sons, 1914), p. 161.

21. *A Statement of Facts Respecting the School for Colored Females in Canterbury, Connecticut, together with a Report of the Late Trial of Miss Prudence Crandall* (Brooklyn, Connecticut, Advertiser Press, 1833). Also *Report of the Arguments of Counsel in Case of Prudence Crandall, Plaintiff in Error, vs. State of Connecticut, Before the Supreme Court of Errors, in July, 1834* (Boston, Garrison & Knapp, 1834).

and this led Miss Crandall at last to give up the idea of continuing the institution. It should be noted in passing, however, that fifty years after this incident the Connecticut legislature voted Miss Crandall a pension of four hundred dollars.[22] It is clear from the reports of the trial and of the community reaction to the school that the primary reason for the objection to the school was that the Negro population of the community would be increased and this would mean increased economic competition and responsibility upon the town.

The growth of Negroes culturally and intellectually was also to cause no little concern to those who thought only of the economic advantages of the slave system. For the attitude naturally developed that since educated Negroes tended to lose their complacency with the slave system they were therefore unfit for slavery. They would have preferred to keep the Negro "lost in the fathomless depths of genial illiteracy." It remained, however, for a singular economic event to seal the doom of unhampered education of Negroes in the ante bellum period. Historians have often pointed out that, until the industrial revolution and the invention of the cotton gin, slavery in America was rapidly becoming more of a liability than an asset.[23] Even some Southerners had advocated colonization of Negroes as a solution to the economic problem which their presence presented. The industrial revolution, effective in most of the western world, was characterized by increased efficiency in textile production and resulted in creating a great demand for cotton. Slavery and the plantation system, then, became of major importance in the South. This movement, along with the rise of intelligent Negroes, Negroes who knew something of the French Revolution and of what blacks were doing in Haiti under Toussaint L'Ouverture and who were beginning to promote strong antislavery sentiment, resulted in a strong reaction against Negro education and in stringent measures subsequently being taken against it.[24] As far back as 1740, when South Carolina was still a British province, that state had passed the first legislation prohibiting the instruction of Negroes, making it a crime punishable by a fine of one hundred pounds. The next law was passed by Georgia some thirty years later, but most of such legislation came after the firm economic reëstablishment of slavery in the first forty years of the nineteenth century.[25] Woodson sums up the situation as follows:

The States attacked the problem in various ways. Colored people beyond a certain number were not allowed to assemble for social or religious purposes, unless in the presence of certain "discreet" white men; slaves were

22. Clark, *op. cit.*, pp. 162–163.
23. Gallagher, *op. cit.*, p. 37.
24. Woodson, *op. cit.*, p. 8.
25. C. S. Johnson, *op. cit.*, p. 226.

deprived of the helpful contacts with free persons of color driving them out of some Southern States; masters who had employed their favorite blacks in positions which required knowledge of bookkeeping, printing, and the like, were commanded by law to discontinue that custom; and private and public teachers were prohibited from assisting Negroes to acquire knowledge in any manner whatever.[26]

From this time until after the Civil War, the majority of the Negroes in America were deprived of educational advantages. As pointed out above, however, some of the slave owners in the South defied the laws and continued to educate the slaves, believing that the economic life of the South would be helped thereby. Many of the slaves were trained to do skilled labor such as brick masonry and carpentry. In order to maintain the economic efficiency of this group and thus to gain added profit from their slaves, the masters, sometimes secretly, sometimes defiantly, disregarded the laws prohibiting the instruction of slaves.[27]

Effect of the Civil War upon Negro education. Properly speaking, the real task of Negro education began with the close of the Civil War and the freedom of the more than 4,000,000 slaves who were thus ushered into a new life. There was now posed the gigantic problem of the rehabilitation of the South, the reëstablishment of orderly government, and the satisfactory assimilation of the new citizens. What kind of education should the freedmen have now that they were accorded full legal status of citizenship?

Bond estimated that in the slave states at the time of the Civil War "hardly more than five per cent of the Negro population possessed the simplest tools of learning." [28] This means obviously that the first task in Negro education in this period was the provision of the necessary tool subjects upon which the superstructure of secondary and higher education should be founded.

Another primary fact which helped to determine educational provisions for the Negro at the time of emancipation was his need of economic security. It was soon realized that the task of reconstruction in the former slave states involved the reconstruction of life habits and patterns of thought of the former slaves as well as of their former masters. Where the Negro previously had practically nothing to do with providing for his own basic needs—food, shelter, clothing—now he was suddenly thrown upon his own resources and was compelled to shift for himself as a free citizen.

The educational work of the Freedmen's Bureau. The agency which played the most significant role in aiding the Negro toward his proper

26. Woodson, *op. cit.*, pp. 8–9.
27. H. M. Bond, *op. cit.*, p. 21.
28. *Ibid.*

social adjustments in this early period was the Freedmen's Bureau of the Federal Government. Not long after the outbreak of the Civil War the Negro was considered as a special ward of the Federal Government. It was Gen. Benjamin F. Butler of Fortress Monroe, Virginia, who solved the problem of what disposition should be made of the slaves who either ran away from their masters or were captured from them by declaring that the slaves were "contraband of War." [29] As the number of slaves who came under the protection of the Union Army increased so did the problem of their care increase. Eventually their care was entrusted to the Union generals. In the meantime certain of the religious denominations went to work on the problem and established schools for the slaves.

Until the act establishing the Freedmen's Bureau finally became a law, the Federal provision for the slave's social welfare did not become effectively organized. In the second session of the Thirty-eighth Congress, William D. Kelly, in a speech advocating the establishment of the Freedmen's Bureau, made the following assertion which shows some of the objectives of the Bureau.

Mr. Speaker, it is not often given to a legislature to perform an act such as we are now to pass upon. We have four million people in poverty because our laws have denied them the right to acquire property; in ignorance because our laws made it a felony to instruct them; without organized habits because war has broken the shackles which bound them; and has released them from the plantations which were destined to be their world.

We are to organize them into a society; we are to guide them, as the guardian guides his ward, for a brief period, until they can acquire habits and become confident and capable of self-control; we are to watch over them, and if we do, we have, from their conduct in the field and in the school, evidence that they will more than repay our labor. If we do not, we will doom them to vagrancy and pauperism, and throw upon another Congress, and perhaps another generation, the duty or the effort to reclaim those whose hopes we will have blasted, whose usefulness we will have destroyed.[30]

There was no unanimity of opinion in Congress with reference to this matter. On March 3, 1865, however, after much heated discussion, the bill finally became a law.[31]

The act gave judicial as well as legislative authority and executive authority to a commissioner over more than four million Negroes. In time, considerable financial and economic resources were also placed at his disposal.

29. Holmes, *op. cit.*, pp. 22–23.
30. Quoted in *ibid.*, pp. 31–32.
31. *Ibid.*, p. 33.

The first commissioner was General O. O. Howard, who established headquarters in Washington and organized the work on the basis of dividing the area under his supervision into districts. In view of the fact that the original act establishing the Bureau did not include provisions for education, General Howard sought to have an amendment made that would make it possible to carry out this phase of the work. After some difficulty an amendment was finally passed in July, 1866, over the veto of President Johnson, authorizing the Bureau to include education as one of its functions. Later, as the missionary education moved on apace under the military protection of the Union soldiers and as the federal and state educational opportunities increased, intimidation and active opposition arose, spear-headed largely by the Ku-Klux Klan. Yet, in spite of this difficulty, the movement for the education of the Negro went forward.

One of the most important features of the work of the Freedmen's Bureau was the aid given in the establishment and maintenance of the schools founded under denominational auspices. Of the several colleges helped between 1865 and 1871 more than twelve are now in operation as permanent institutions. Chief among these is Howard University, named in honor of Gen. O. O. Howard. It was founded in 1867 to help meet the need of supplying teachers, preachers, and other leaders for the freedmen. As originally stated, the aim of this institution was "the education of the colored youth for the ministry." [32] This school rose rapidly to first rank among Negro institutions of higher learning. Others of similar rank established in this period are Fisk University, Nashville, Tennessee, and Atlanta University, Atlanta, Georgia. According to one of the early catalogues of Howard University, the requirements for admission to the college were as follows:

. . . two books of Caesar, six orations of Cicero, the Bucolics, the Georgics, six books of Vergil's Aeneid, and Sallust's Cataline, two books of Xenophon's Anabasis, and the first two books of Homer's Illiad. In addition to these requirements, the student was required to pass examinations in higher arithmetic, algebra to quadratics, the history of Greece and Rome, ancient and modern geography, and English grammar.[33]

These requirements were essentially the same as those for admission to the traditional white colleges of the nation. Since 1879 Congress has regularly appropriated funds to Howard University. Today around 50 per cent of its total budget comes from the Federal Government.

Educational philosophy during the Civil War period. It should be borne in mind that throughout this period of educational expansion for Negroes

32. *Ibid.*, p. 50.
33. *Ibid.*, p. 54.

there was much conflict of opinion with reference to how far beyond the mere fundamentals of learning, if even to this extent, Negro education should go. Two or three different schools of thought are observed. In the first place, as already indicated, there was open hostility on the part of certain whites in the South to Negro education. The ignorant whites of the South opposed Negro education because they themselves had not the advantages of education and, besides, education had previously been the privilege of the wealthy, slave-owning minority. Others felt that, inasmuch as the Negro had as a slave done all the laborious tasks in the economic and social set-up, so even now as a freedman his place in society should be largely that of a common laborer. Some more enlightened Southerners believed that Negroes should receive an education, but they were quite wary of the kind of education which the Northern missionaries were bringing. They resented, among other things, the assumption of social equality implied in giving Negroes the same kind of training that whites received.

On the other hand, the Northern philanthropists, for the most part filled with zeal to right the wrongs of slavery and to help the Negro to rise high in the scale of development, advocated strongly the same kind of education for the Negroes that whites had. The dominant education in America had been based on the classics and rooted in the culture of the past. Harvard, Yale, and Princeton, each of the latter two called the "mother of colleges," set the standard for education in America. There were a good many people, therefore, who held that the education of the freedmen should follow the pattern set by those older institutions. The Northern missionaries set about establishing colleges and universities even though these at the outset were for the most part universities only in name. In spite of the fact that the primary task of these schools was to provide elementary and secondary education, the ultimate objective was the traditional "liberal education" on the higher levels that differed little if at all from that of the white institutions.

In some notable instances this philosophy of education and the consequent practices have been severely criticized by Negroes as well as whites. J. L. M. Curry, a prominent Southern white man interested in the welfare of the Negro, indicted the early education of the Negro in this period in these words:

The education was unsettling, demoralizing, pandered to a wild frenzy for schooling as a quick method of reversing social and political conditions. Nothing could have been better devised for deluding the poor Negro, and making him the tool, the slave of corrupt taskmasters. . . . The curriculum was for a people in the highest degree of civilization; the aptitude and capabilities and needs of the Negro were wholly disregarded.[34]

34. Quoted in *ibid.*, pp. 44–45.

Another opinion along the same line should be noted. This comes from an outstanding sociologist, E. B. Reuter.

The work of even the best schools conducted along sectarian and classical lines was barren of results; they contributed practically nothing to the real education of the Negroes nor to the improvement of the social and economic conditions of the race. The whole movement, particularly the bringing of Northern Negro churches into the South, widened the breach between the races, intensified race hatred and increased the social and cultural isolation of Negroes.[35]

On the other hand, others, such as Kelly Miller and W. E. B. Du Bois, were strongly in favor of the type of instruction which was given Negroes in this early period. Miller, for example, favored it on the grounds that this type of education was needed to bring the Negro up to his fullest capacity for moral and spiritual development, without which, he thought, Negroes could not hope to make real progress. Miller said, "The ability to saw to a line or hit a nail aplomb with a hammer does not create a zeal for righteousness and truth. It is only when the pupil comes to feel the vitalizing power of knowledge that it begins to react upon the life and fructify in character." [36]

Du Bois for a long time was the most articulate champion of this early type of instruction for Negroes. Writing on "The Talented Tenth," he justifies classical instruction of Negroes on such grounds as these:

All men cannot go to college, but some men must; every isolated group or nation must have its yeast, must have for the talented a few centers of training where men are not so mystified and befuddled by the hard and necessary toil of earning a living as to have no aims higher than their bellies, and no God greater than gold. This is true training, and thus in the beginning were the favored sons of the freedmen trained.[37]

For a long time the two symbols of the dilemma of which kind of education Negroes should have were Du Bois and Booker T. Washington, the latter perhaps the most outstanding educator the race has produced. Du Bois was often quite bitter in his objections to Washington's educational philosophy and practice, yet, in establishing and carrying forward the vocational work of Tuskegee Institute, Washington was eminently successful. There can be no doubt that one explanation of the financial support which Tuskegee and Hampton have received through the years is that many whites would more gladly support the "education of the Negro's hand" rather than his head.

Religious organizations and denominations in the development of Ne-

35. *Holmes, op. cit.,* p. 72.
36. *Ibid.*
37. *Ibid.,* p. 73.

gro education after the Civil War. Had it not been for the various religious organizations that became fired with a tremendous zeal for the education of the freedmen, it is hard to imagine what would now be the intellectual and social status of the race. The establishment and maintenance of schools and colleges on a large scale after the War between the States constitutes one of the most important chapters in the history of American education.

The first organization in the field was the American Missionary Association, organized in 1846. Basic in its philosophy was a strict belief in the democratic principles of the equality of all men before God and the injustice of the slave system. Out of the efforts of this organization grew the help given in the formation of Berea College in Kentucky, a college organized in 1858 for the "co-education of the races." As stated in the first by-law of this college organization, "The object of this college shall be to furnish the facilities for thorough education of all persons of good moral character." But the second by-law read, "This college shall be under an influence strictly Christian, and as such opposed to sectarianism, slave-holding, caste, and every other wrong institution or practice." [38] Unfortunately, after a legal fight which eventually went to the Supreme Court of the United States, Berea College was forced in 1904 to abandon its practice of inter-racial education. Faced with this necessity, the college authorities made a division of the funds of the school and established a separate school for Negroes named Lincoln University, twenty-two miles from the city of Louisville, Kentucky. [39]

In 1861 the American Missionary Association opened a weekday school in Fortress Monroe, Virginia. This school began in September of that year with twenty pupils, which number was soon augmented to fifty. "The evidences of the aptitude of the children to learn, and the desire of adults for knowledge were strikingly manifest. Elementary books and the materials for instruction were provided, and the work went forward with cheering results." [40] This school later moved to nearby Hampton in 1868. The association carried on work in other towns of the Hampton Roads area.

Hampton Institute was chartered as a college in 1870 and it soon became the headquarters for the training of Negro teachers in Virginia. Gen. Samuel C. Armstrong, the first principal of this school, conceived as its objectives,

. . . to train selected Negro youth who should go out to teach and lead their people, first by example, by getting land and homes; to give them

38. Quoted in *ibid.*, p. 73.
39. Interview with President W. J. Hutchins of Berea College.
40. American Missionary Association, *Sixteenth Annual Report* (New York, American Missionary Association, 1862), p. 39.

not a dollar that they could not earn themselves; to teach respect for labor; to replace stupid drudgery with skilled hands; and to these ends to build up an industrial system for the sake, not only of self-respect and intelligent labor, but also for the sake of character.[41]

In the meantime other permanent institutions for the education of Negroes were being established by the American Missionary Association. Fisk University was chartered in 1867 in Nashville, Tennessee. The president of that institution reported in 1871 that there were 524 pupils enrolled from nine different states. "We have four pupils," he said, "who are just ready for college." [42]

Atlanta University was also chartered in 1867 under the auspices of the association. In 1871 there were 158 pupils reported. One pupil in the senior class was said to be "well fitted to enter college this fall." [43] An indication of the reaction of some of the Southern people to this school is seen in this item from the newspaper, the *Atlanta Constitution*, which appeared in one of its editions in June, 1871.

The exercises in Atlanta (colored) University during the present week have been exceedingly interesting, as they are something novel in this section of the country.

We were not prepared for what we witnessed. To see colored boys and girls between fourteen and eighteen years of age, reciting in Greek and Latin, and demonstrating correctly problems in Algebra and geometry, and seemingly understanding what they demonstrated, appears almost wonderful. . . . Some of the most genuine proficient and advanced scholars, strange as it may seem, are genuine coal-black Africans.[44]

Several other schools and colleges were founded by or with the coöperation of the association, including Talladega College, Alabama, Tillotson College, Texas, and Tougaloo College, Mississippi.

While the concern of the Baptist denomination for the welfare of the Negro was doubtless demonstrated in several isolated instances prior to the Civil War, the group as a whole apparently took no concerted action with respect to alleviating the conditions of the slaves until about the time of the civil strife. The American Baptist Home Mission Society was founded in 1832 "to promote the preaching of the Gospel in North America.[45] A canvass of the majority of the annual reports of this society from the time of its founding until the outbreak of the Civil War reveals no mention of any work being carried on in the interest of the slaves. At the

41. Holmes, *op. cit.*, p. 85.
42. American Missionary Association, *Twenty-fifth Annual Report* (New York, American Missionary Association, 1871), p. 38.
43. *Ibid.*, p. 41.
44. *Ibid.*
45. American Baptist Home Mission Society, *Tenth Annual Report* (New York, American Baptist Home Mission Society, 1842), p. 2.

annual meeting of the society in 1862 its "Committee on the Occupation of Southern Fields," after taking cognizance of the abolition of slavery in the District of Columbia and other places and feeling that "Divine Hand most distinctly and most imperatively beckoning us on to the occupancy of a field broader, more important and more promising than has ever yet invited our toils," made the following resolutions,

That we recommend the Society to take immediate steps to supply with Christian instruction, by means of missionaries and teachers, the emancipated slaves—whether in the District of Columbia or in other places now held by our forces—and also to inaugurate a system of operations for carrying the Gospel alike to free and bond throughout the whole southern section of our country, so fast and so far as the progress of our arms, and the restoration of order and law shall open the way.[46]

Subsequent to this action the work of the Baptists of the North rapidly increased and expanded. Much of the zeal of this group for the education of the freedmen was inspired by the fact that the majority of the latter were Baptists either in affiliation or in inclination. The major emphasis in the Baptist mission to the Negroes was the training of preachers who would be the spiritual leaders of their race. Funds for these efforts increased with remarkable rapidity. In 1871 it was reported that 2,768 persons had been given instructions by missionary teachers in weekday schools and classes and that the property value of the seven schools conducted under the auspices of the Society at that time totaled $130,000.[47] By 1884 the Baptists had established a total of fifteen Negro and two Indian schools with a total property valuation of $500,000.[48] The majority of these schools are still in operation.

Following the Civil War the Methodist Episcopal Church, from which the Southern branch had separated over the question of slavery in 1844, began a series of activities which was to culminate in extensive work being done on behalf of the freedmen. The work centered in the Freedmen's Aid Society of the Methodist Episcopal Church, which was organized in 1866. The object of this organization was "the relief and uplifting of Freedmen through Christian education." [49] Starting out with the sense of responsibility to do something significant in the name of the denomination, in six years the Freedmen's Society had spent $300,000 for the various educational enterprises among the Negroes, of which $150,000 was invested in school property.[50] By the year 1877 there were 16 institutions of higher learning reported with an estimated 1,500 pupils taught

46. *Ibid., Thirtieth Annual Report* (New York, 1862), pp. 50–51.
47. *Ibid., Thirty-ninth Annual Report* (New York, 1871), p. 26.
48. *Ibid., Fifty-second Annual Report* (New York, 1884), p. 58.
49. Thomas H. Pearne, "The Freedmen," *Methodist Quarterly Review*, LIX (January, 1877), 472–473.
50. *Ibid.*

by 26 teachers.[51] By this time the society had spent $1,290,363 in the interest of the development of the freedmen. Among the permanent schools established are Clark College, Georgia, Wiley College, Texas, and Bennett College, North Carolina.

Through the "Presbyterian Committee of Missions to Freedmen," the Presbyterian Church in the United States began in 1865 to carry on systematic constructive work among Southern Negroes. The object of this committee was "to cultivate piety among the Freedmen by planting and maintaining among them the Church and School conjointly, that is, carrying forward in the same place a church and day-school." [52] Seven years after its organization the committee reported the organization and maintenance of 39 day schools and 5 higher schools. These latter had a total property valuation of $40,000. Johnson C. Smith University, North Carolina, and Lincoln University, Pennsylvania, are the outstanding permanent contributions of the work of this group. The Board of Freedmen's Missions of the United Presbyterian Church also was active in the field of Negro education but their work was not quite so extensive as that of some of the larger groups. Knoxville College, Tennessee, founded in 1875, represents the outstanding contribution of this branch of the Presbyterian movement.

Other religious groups representing Northern philanthropy active in the organization and maintenance of Negro schools and colleges were the Society of Friends, the Episcopalians, the Disciples, Adventists, and Catholics. Most of the Catholic schools were on the elementary or secondary level. Incidentally, the one outstanding college for Negroes supported by the Catholic Church in America is Xavier University, New Orleans, Louisiana, founded in 1915.

It should be remembered also that the Negro churches themselves sought to do something about the education of the members of the race. Pioneering among them was the African Methodist Episcopal Church, organized in 1819. Six permanent colleges were established by this denomination between 1870 and 1886.[53] Wilberforce University, since 1856 under the auspices of the A.M.E. Church, is the second oldest Negro institution in America, Lincoln University, Pennsylvania, antedating it by two years. An indication of the educational activity of the principal Negro church groups since the Civil War is given in statistics made available in 1916.[54] According to these figures, there was a total of 153 schools maintained by Negro denominational boards in 1916, of which 60 were considered "large or important" and 93 as "small or less important schools."

51. *Ibid.*, p. 475.
52. *Ibid.*, p. 470.
53. Holmes, *op. cit.*, p. 144.
54. T. J. Jones, *op. cit.*, I, 344–346.

Of the 153 schools, 110 were maintained by Baptists, having a total enrollment of 11,250. The African Methodist Episcopal Church maintained 17 schools with a total enrollment of 3,312 students. Thirteen of these schools were considered to be of special significance while only four were said to be relatively unimportant. At the same time, the African Methodist Episcopal Zion Church maintained 11 schools, and the Colored Methodist Episcopal Church supported a total of 9. The 153 schools supported by colored denominational boards reported a combined income for current expenses of $380,933 for 1916. While it is difficult to understand how as many schools as there were could be adequately supported on this small amount, the striking fact is that out of the meager resources of the underprivileged race so much money could be invested in educational enterprises.

Only a small portion of these 153 schools were offering college work. In fact, there were only 33 schools giving any work at all in college courses. In these 33 institutions, 1,643 students were enrolled in college courses and 994 were enrolled in professional courses. The remaining 10,089 pupils which these colleges reported were in the secondary and elementary grades.[55]

The Morrill Land-Grant Acts. The passing of the Morrill Land-Grant Acts facilitated in a large way the development of Negro education. Federal funds were set aside for the establishment of agricultural and mechanical colleges for Negroes in the Southern states. These states, however, were slow in making adequate use of these funds. Only four states in the South made any provisions for the equitable distribution of the sums received between 1862 and 1890. In this latter year special stipulations were set forth in the act to the effect that states with segregated systems of education should divide the funds equitably. Until 1916 these schools offered no work of collegiate grade.

Philanthropy in Negro education. The story of the development of higher education among Negroes is not complete without some consideration of the various philanthropic agencies that either directly or indirectly have promoted the progress of the colleges.

The John F. Slater Fund of $1,000,000 was established in 1882. Mr. Slater, a merchant of Norwich, Connecticut, made the following statement in a letter setting forth his purpose in establishing the fund:

The general object which I desire to have exclusively pursued, is the uplifting of the lately emancipated population of the Southern states, and their posterity, by conferring on them the blessing of Christian education. The disabilities formerly suffered by these people, and their singular patience and fidelity in the great crisis of the nation, establish a just claim on the sympathy and good will of humane and patriotic men. I cannot but

55. *Ibid.,* I, 59.

feel the compassion that is due in view of their prevailing ignorance which exists by no fault of their own.

But it is not only for their own sake, but also for the safety of our common country, in which they have been invested with equal political rights, that I am desirous to aid in providing them with the means of such education as shall tend to make them good men and good citizens—education in which the instruction of the mind in the common branches of secular learning shall be associated with training in just notions of duty toward God and man, in the light of the Holy Scriptures.[56]

This fund has granted more than $2,000,000 to Negro colleges and universities.

The Anna T. Jeanes Fund was established by a Quaker lady of that name and was devoted to the development of rural Negro schools. The George Peabody Fund of $1,000,000 was established for "the promotion of and encouragement of intellectual, moral, or industrial education among the youth of the more destitute portions of the Southern and Southwestern states of our Union; my purpose being that the benefits intended shall be distributed among the entire population, without other distinction than their needs and the opportunities of usefulness to them.[57]

The work of the Julius Rosenwald Fund has resulted in better rural schools for Negroes and also, through direct contributions to colleges for the promotion of research, it has helped them to lift and to maintain high standards of educational activities. The General Education Board, incorporated in 1903, has been the agency of the Rockefeller family in granting aid to education. Negro colleges have received aid for endowments, study leaves for teachers, and other purposes from this fund. One other large agency, the Phelps-Stokes Fund, established in 1910, has made contributions to Negro education in various ways, one of the most important of which has been as a bureau for the gathering and dissemination of information on Negro education. Obviously, without the aid of such private philanthropy, Negro higher education would have been slower in reaching its present status.[58]

The present status of Negro higher education. The present situation in higher education among Negroes reflects the significant progress which has been made since 1865. In 1936 it was estimated that 37,397 persons had been graduated from Negro institutions. This represents 83.3 per cent of the 43,821 Negro graduates from all colleges in the nation since Bowdoin graduated the first Negro in America in 1826.[59] It cannot

56. Quoted in Holmes, *op. cit.*, p. 166.

57. *Ibid.*, p. 156.

58. U. W. Leavell, *Philanthropy in Negro Education* (Nashville, George Peabody College for Teachers, 1930), p. 167.

59. C. S. Johnson, *The Negro College Graduate* (Chapel Hill, University of North Carolina Press, 1938), p. 10.

be said that the situation now is ideal by any means, but, measured in terms of the relatively short time in which they have been operating, the colleges have made significant progress despite tremendous handicaps.

Although some claim a larger number, there are at least 108 Negro institutions offering collegiate instruction.[60] Table I shows the distribu-

TABLE I
CONTROL OF HIGHER EDUCATION AMONG NEGROES *

Type of Institution	State	District or Municipal	Private	Denomi-national	Total
College or University	15	2	6	38	61
Professional School	1	–	4	2	7
Teachers College	9	3	–	–	12
Normal School	–	–	1	3	4
Junior College	6	1	3	14	24
Grand Total	31	6	14	57	108

* This table is adapted from the *Educational Directory*, United States Office of Education Bulletin, 1940, No. 1, Part III (Washington, United States Government Printing Office, 1940), p. 7.

tion of these 108 colleges according to type of control. It will be seen that 37 or approximately 34 per cent of the Negro colleges are under public control, while the remaining 66 per cent are either under private or denominational control. The 57 schools under denominational control are distributed among 12 denominational agencies. Table II shows the dis-

TABLE II
DENOMINATIONAL CONTROL OF 57 NEGRO COLLEGES *

Baptist	16
Methodist	8
African Methodist Episcopal	6
Presbyterian, U.S.A.	6
Colored Methodist Episcopal	5
American Missionary Association (Congregational)	4
African Methodist Episcopal Zion	2
Episcopal	5
Disciples	2
United Presbyterian	1
Roman Catholic	1
Seventh Day Adventist	1
Total	57

* Statistics taken from *Educational Directory*, United States Office of Education Bulletin, 1940, No. 1, Part III (Washington, United States Government Printing Office, 1940), pp. 9 ff.

60. *Educational Directory*, United States Office of Education Bulletin, 1940, No. 1, Part III (Washington, United States Government Printing Office, 1940), p. 7.

tribution of Negro higher educational institutions according to denominational control. Since the largest percentage of Negroes are either of the Baptist or of the Methodist faith, it is no more than natural that, as Table II reveals, the largest number of denominational colleges should be controlled by these groups. Sixteen, or 28 per cent, of the 57 institutions are under the control of Baptist groups. Eight, or 14 per cent, are under the control of the Methodist Episcopal Church, while 13 others are under the control of the other branches of Methodism supported by Negroes. Thus a total of 21, or 36 per cent, of the denominational institutions among Negroes are under the control of some branch of the Methodist Church. The Baptists and the Methodists, therefore, control a total of 37 institutions among Negroes giving collegiate instruction, or 65 per cent of the total number of church-related schools.

Denominational preferences of students. For the purpose of the present study, questionnaires were sent to the registrars of 104 Negro higher institutions requesting the information on the denominational preferences of their students as of the school year 1940–41. Forty-three, or 42 per cent, of the schools supplied data. The total enrollment of the schools responding was 20,065, which is approximately 50 per cent of the total Negro college population. Of the total number of students from the colleges from which statistics are available, 8,454, or 42 per cent, were listed as members of the Baptist Church, as Table III indicates. The next larg-

TABLE III

DENOMINATIONAL PREFERENCES OF NEGRO COLLEGE
STUDENTS IN 43 COLLEGES ARRANGED BY TYPE OF COLLEGE

Denomination		Total	Type of College		
			Church	Private	Public
Baptists		8,454	2,517	1,693	4,244
Methodists		6,386			
Methodist	2,901		1,181	272	1,448
African Methodist Episcopal	2,408		911	523	974
African Methodist Episcopal Zion	608		223	30	355
Colored Methodist Episcopal	469		79	253	137
Presbyterians		915	403	131	381
Catholic		831	168	187	476
Episcopal		640	136	221	283
Congregational-Christian		289	82	57	150
Others		841	340	135	366
Non-church		1,064	237	248	579
No information		645	95	136	414
Total		20,065	6,372	3,886	9,807

est denominational group was the Methodists, with as many as 31 per cent of the students of this study reported as being members of some branch of this Wesleyan organization. The largest percentage of Methodists was to be found in the Methodist Church and next to it in number of student adherents was the African Methodist Episcopal Church. It is significant that only 5 per cent of the students regarding whom statistics are available were reported as having no church affiliation.

In Table IV are given the results of a national survey of the church

TABLE IV

DENOMINATIONAL PREFERENCES OF STUDENTS ACCORDING TO A NATIONAL SURVEY, 1936–37 *

Denomination	Number of Students Showing Preference
Methodist	156,423
Catholic, Roman	122,786
Baptist	99,219
Presbyterian	88,473
Christian-Congregational	48,354
Episcopal, Protestant	47,729
Lutheran	38,339
Hebrew	32,405
Disciples of Christ	13,921
Christian Science	12,282
Latter Day Saints	11,428
Reformed	5,194
Adventist, Seventh Day	4,620
Evangelical	4,104
Unitarian	3,297
United Brethren	3,226
Friends	2,496
Brethren	1,990
Church of God	1,861
Evangelical-Reformed	1,454
Mennonite	1,335
Universalist	1,051
Baptist, Seventh Day	903
Moravian	796
Others	26,946
No Preference	45,906
No Information	51,533
Total	828,071

* Gould Wickey, "A National Survey of the Religious Preferences of Students in American Colleges and Universities, 1936–37," *Christian Education*, XXI, No. 1 (October, 1937), 52.

preferences of college students.[61] When these figures are compared with those just given for Negro students, some striking variations are observed. In the first place, while 42 per cent of the Negro students belonged to the Baptist faith, only 12 per cent of the total number of students in the national survey were of this affiliation. Secondly, the largest number of students in the national study, 19 per cent, belonged to the Methodist Church, as compared with 31 per cent of the Negro students studied separately. Again, the second largest number of students in the national survey belonging to a single communion were members of the Catholic church. Of the 828,071 students of this study, 14 per cent were Catholics. In the separate study of Negro students it was found that only 4 per cent were Catholics. It is also to be observed that there are relatively few denominational groups among Negroes as compared with figures for the nation as a whole.

Clergymen as college presidents. In connection with the study of the denominational preferences of Negro college students, information was also sought regarding the number of presidents of Negro institutions who were licensed or ordained ministers. Of the 43 institutions reporting, 17, or 40 per cent, indicated that the president was an ordained or licensed clergyman. The majority of these, of course, were in the church-related institutions. The presidents of 14 of the 19 church-related colleges reporting were ministers of religion, whereas only 2 licensed or ordained ministers were found to be presidents of tax-supported colleges, and 1 private institution reported having a minister as its president. These figures are evidence that to a large extent still the forces of organized religion are concerned about having religious leaders as administrators of institutions of higher learning among Negroes.

Enrollment. Complete statistics of enrollment in the 108 colleges listed in the 1940 *Educational Directory* are not available. In response to the inquiry concerning enrollment as well as denominational affiliation, 43 out of 104 institutions from which information was requested reported a total enrollment of 20,030 students. Since the majority of the larger colleges responded to this inquiry, it is doubtless true that this number represents more than 50 per cent of the total enrollment in Negro colleges. A survey of 66 degree-granting institutions for Negroes conducted by the *Crisis* magazine in August, 1941, revealed a total of 37,203 students enrolled.[62] On the basis of these two surveys it is probable that the total enrollment of students in colleges for Negroes as of 1940–41 is hardly more than 40,000.

In a study of 117 Negro institutions of higher learning in 1931–32,

61. Gould Wickey, *op. cit.*, pp. 49–55.
62. "The American Negro in College," *The Crisis*, XLVIII (August, 1941), 251–252.

there was reported a total of 38,274 students enrolled.[63] Of this number, 19,037 were enrolled in private and denominational schools while 19,237 were enrolled in schools under public control. Thus, although the public institutions constituted only 30 per cent of the total number of schools, they enrolled in 1931–32 slightly more than 50 per cent of the entire number of students in all the colleges. This means that the 36 public colleges had an average enrollment of 534 students while the 81 private and denominational colleges had an average attendance of only 235 students each.

Standardization. Relatively few of the Negro colleges have become sufficiently standardized to receive the highest accreditation of their regional accrediting agency. Of 88 institutions in 11 states reported by the Southern Association of Colleges and Secondary Schools in 1938, only 19, or 22 per cent, had been given Class A rating, although 24 others had been given Class B rating.[64]

Finance. Statistics for 1935–36 show that 87 Negro institutions of higher learning reported the value of buildings and grounds to be $62,926,300. In the same year the total number of bound volumes in the libraries of 90 institutions was given as 1,062,155.[65] Incidentally, the combined number of volumes in the libraries of these 90 institutions was somewhat less than the total number of volumes in the Sterling Memorial Library in Yale University, which, in 1940, amounted to 2,219,000.[66] In 1935–36, 93 institutions reported total revenue receipts of $13,140,721 while at the same time 89 institutions reported expenditures amounting to $13,006,075.[67] Forty-one institutions reported endowment funds amounting to $36,533,830.[68]

Some conclusions. The present status of higher education among Negroes, while not ideal, indicates the importance which religious and philanthropic agencies still have in the advancement of Negroes. With more than 70 per cent of the total number of colleges for Negroes, having an enrollment of approximately half of the Negro collegiate population, controlled by religious agencies, it is clear that the place which religion has held and still holds in higher education among Negroes is one of strategic importance. At the same time, the fact that half of the Negro college students are enrolled in tax-supported institutions poses a problem

63. D. A. Wilkerson, *Special Problems of Negro Education* (Washington, United States Government Printing Office, 1939), p. 61.

64. *Ibid.,* p. 71.

65. Blose, David, and Caliver, Ambrose, *Statistics of the Education of Negroes,* United States Office of Education Bulletin, 1938, No. 13 (Washington, United States Government Printing Office, 1939), p. 17.

66. Yale University, *Catalogue,* 1940–41, p. 209.

67. Blose and Caliver, *op. cit.,* p. 17.

68. *Ibid.*

for those interested in the place of religion in the education of youth. For, unless such considerations as the development of an adequate world view, life philosophy, and compelling spiritual ideals appear in the curriculum of Negro youth, the future educational program of this group will have little real meaning.

II

THE RELATION OF RELIGION TO THE SOCIAL SETTING AND THE OBJECTIVES OF HIGHER EDUCATION AMONG NEGROES

THE historical background of higher education among Negroes reflects at once the influence of religious forces in that education as well as the various phenomena of a caste society which at every point help to condition it. To be realistic, a philosophy for the religious program of the Negro college will take cognizance, among other things, of the social setting in which the educational process is carried on. The religious program of the college must relate itself to the social and psychological factors which serve to determine the personality development of Negro students. But, not only the religious program but the entire scheme of the objectives of the college will be determined in large part by the kind of society in which the students live and into which they must go after leaving the college.

A series of studies have appeared recently which have searchingly brought out many of the social and psychological problems which Negro youth face.[1] While these studies are related primarily to the problems of youth on the elementary and high school levels, they do serve to make clear some of the major forces with which educational philosophy must concern itself if it is to be realistic. The matter of the relation of the school to society is particularly apropos in any discussion of education of a minority group. The impact of environmental forces upon a social minority is often severe.

It will be instructive, therefore, to see the implications which the caste status of Negroes in America has for the education of this group in general and for their religious education in particular. As will be soon demonstrated, this is one of the most important factors to be considered in the entire program of Negro education in America. Several writers have drawn attention to the relevancy of this problem to Negro life and education.[2]

1. John Dollard, *Caste and Class in a Southern Town* (New Haven, Yale University Press, 1937) ; Allison Davis and John Dollard, *Children of Bondage* (Washington, American Council on Education, 1940) ; C. S. Johnson, *Growing Up in the Black Belt* (Washington, American Council on Education, 1940) ; E. F. Frazier, *Negro Youth at the Crossways* (Washington, American Council on Education, 1940). W. Lloyd Warner *et al.*, *Color and Human Nature* (Washington, American Council on Education, 1941).

2. W. Lloyd Warner, "American Caste and Class," *American Journal of Sociology,*

The racial situation in America, particularly in the states where the majority of Negro colleges are located, is one which does not allow every person to rise to the limit of his possibilities even if he has the urge to do so. The great obstacles are the barriers of both caste and class. It is assumed that through initiative and achievement a person may break through class lines, or through loss of these factors he may lose whatever status he may have. But it is never assumed that one may transcend his caste. Within the white and Negro castes which characterize American life, there are various classes, but between these two castes there is a rigid wall beyond which society does not countenance communciation on a basis of equality.

The rise of caste in America may be attributed to several factors, chief among which is the former slave status of the Negro. In the plantation South Negroes had a life on the whole not quite as idyllic as some reports of the slave system may lead one to believe. As a slave the Negro was considered in much the same terms as the other property of the master class and was often treated as less than human.

The slave system itself was a mixed blessing to the majority of the whites of the South. It has been pointed out in recent studies that the large majority of the whites of the old South belonged to the economically insecure class, and that only 30 per cent of the whites belonged to the wealthy, slaveholding aristocracy. This meant that the white majority were deprived of many economic opportunities that they would have had under a free rather than a slaveholding economy. The result of this situation was that there grew up a strong prejudice and hatred toward the Negro on the part of the whites, a feeling which was intensified by the events of the Reconstruction era and which resulted in the most stringent measures being taken against the Negro, many of which have survived to the present day.[3] It is always well to bear in mind that the primary cause of opposition and prejudice on the part of whites toward the Negro was and still remains an economic one, although there are many people who do not realize that this underlies their attitude. This is not to say that other factors such as differences of race or color and previous condition of servitude do not enter into the situation. But it is generally agreed that underlying the prejudice, the oppression and suppression is the fear of economic competition with Negroes on the part of the white majority.

Economic handicaps in the environment. Today there are certain types of employment which the Negro may not hope to enter. He is restricted

---

LXII (September, 1936), 234–237. D. A. Wilkerson, "American Caste and the Social Studies Curriculum," *Quarterly Review of Higher Education among Negroes*, V (April, 1937), 67–74. B. G. Gallagher, *American Caste and the Negro College* (New York, Columbia University Press, 1938).

3. Dollard, *op. cit.*, p. 59.

for the most part to the unskilled or menial types of labor. He is therefore on the lowest round of the economic ladder. Even in those occupations traditionally filled by Negroes he no longer has security. It has now
become a truism to say that the Negro is "the last to be hired and the
first to be fired."

This means among other things that the living conditions of Negroes
are quite poor and unsatisfactory. In many cases where the Negro is
crowded into relatively narrow "ghetto" areas as in Harlem, the rental
fees have skyrocketed. The result is gross overcrowding in homes with
its consequent unwholesome health and moral conditions. It is now generally recognized that one of the principal reasons why the tuberculosis
rate is so high among Negroes is that unwholesome living conditions result in their being particularly susceptible to this disease.[4]

Financial status of college students. The Negro student comes to college, therefore, under great material handicaps, due principally to his
background of limited opportunities which result in limited means of
support while in college. A survey of the background of the students in
one small Negro college disclosed that out of the nearly 300 students enrolled, at least 50 per cent came from families whose total income was
$900 or less. Other studies have pointed out similar economic deficiencies
which characterize Negro college students. In a study of undergraduates
at Howard University a few years ago, a school which represents in general students from the more well-to-do families, it was estimated that the
median income of parents was $1,559.52, which is one half the amount of
the median parental income of a group of white students studied in 55
liberal arts colleges.[5] Besides the National Youth Administration, some
schools have set up employment agencies through which a portion of
students are able to get part-time jobs as domestics or as waiters in
hotels.

The psychological effects of caste barriers. In addition to these economic and moral factors playing in upon the environment of Negro youth,
there is a far more subtle set of influences affecting this group. These are
the inimicable racial attitudes and psychological barriers which are usually present, particularly in Southern Negro-white relationships. One of
the most thorough-going studies of how these caste influences operate in
a relatively small Southern town is John Dollard's *Caste and Class in a
Southern Town.* Here the author describes his personal experiences and
investigations in the midst of an acute Negro-white caste situation. A
few quotations from this study will help to demonstrate the attitudes and
racial patterns which generally obtain in the South. In discussing some

4. "Negro Health," *Time Magazine*, XXXV, No. 15 (April 8, 1940), 41.
5. C. S. Johnson, *The Negro College Graduate* (Chapel Hill, University of North
Carolina Press, 1938), p. 10.

psychological concomitants of caste itself, this author makes the following observations:

Caste members tend to develop a distinctive psychology. This is no less true of the white caste than of the Negro, and we must never forget that we have two castes in the South and not just one. Southern white solidarity is caste solidarity. Nor should we overlook the fact that most of us, in the North as well as in the South, are members of the white caste, that we do, in practice, define the Negro as something categorically inferior and demand special privileges for ourselves and fellow whites.[6]

Those who have observed the trend of race relations in America can attest to the truth and significance of this statement. The fact of caste status is one that no Negro (and also no white man) can escape. Dollard puts the matter in the following words:

To the Negro, of course, the caste barrier is an ever-present solid fact. His education is incomplete until he has learned to make some adjustment to it, usually the one preferred by the white caste. Since our democratic society is built on equal opportunity to achieve the highest social distinction, the caste barrier is obviously in contradiction with it. The Negro must haul down his social expectations and resign himself to a relative immobility in contrast to the dominant spirit of our society. This dominant spirit is well expressed by the notion of "beginning at the bottom and working to the top." Moton has pointed out that the Negro may begin at the bottom but, on the average he may expect to stay there, or pretty close to it.[7]

From the point of view of the Negro parent the question becomes particularly acute. In his autobiography, *Along This Way*, James Weldon Johnson depicts something of the problem here.

The question of the child's future is a serious dilemma for Negro parents. Awaiting each colored boy and girl are cramping limitations and buttressed obstacles, in addition to those that must be met by youth in general; and this dilemma approaches suffering in proportion to the parents' knowledge of and the child's innocence of those conditions. Some parents up to the last moment strive to spare the child the bitter knowledge; the child of less sensitive parents is likely to have this knowledge driven in upon him from infancy. And no Negro parent can definitely say which is the wiser course, for either of them may lead to spiritual disaster for the child.[8]

Thus is it obvious that the psychological handicaps of those of the lower caste are quite profound. One of the best discussions of the per-

6. Dollard, *op. cit.*, p. 64.
7. *Ibid.*, pp. 66–67.
8. Quoted in *ibid.*, p. 66, by permission of the Viking Press, New York.

nicious influence of the psychological hazard is given in the remarkable novel by Richard Wright, *Native Son.*[9] Here, with ingenious artistry, the author portrays the tragic life of a Negro youth in a Northern city whose entire soul is perverted by the fact of caste barriers. In trying to explain his attitude toward the situation the main character of the novel, Bigger Thomas, now condemned to die for a purely accidental death of a white girl, makes the following observations: ". . . Jesus, Mr. Max, when folks says things like that about you, you whipped before you born. What's the use? . . . They draw a line and say for you to stay on your side. They don't care if you die. And then they say things like that about you and when you try to come from behind your line they kill you. They feel they ought to kill you then. Everybody wants to kill you then. . . ."[10] Later in the story, the attorney for the condemned youth makes this defense, in part, for his client:

. . . The all-important thing for this Court to remember in deciding this boy's fate is that, though his crime was accidental, the emotions that broke loose were already there; the thing to remember is that this boy's way of life was a way of guilt; that his crime existed long before the murder of Mary Dalton; that the accidental nature of his crime took the guise of a sudden and violent rent in the veil behind which he had lived, a rent which allowed his feelings of resentment and estrangement to leap forth and find objective and concrete form.[11]

It is difficult to measure with precision and accuracy all the psychogenic hazards inherent in the caste system. This novel, however, is an excellent contribution to such understanding.

One thing that should be remembered is that the distortion of mind and soul are not all on the side of the lower caste: the dominant caste itself becomes victimized by its own prejudices and hatreds.[12] The implication of this for the entire educational system is that both Negroes and whites need education that is designed to eliminate those factors in the environment which make for bad personality adjustment.

Gallagher has pointed out four "pathological results" of the caste system as it impinges upon Negroes. In the first place, the Negro may "laugh off" the situation; that is, he may develop the ability to keep his bearings and his cheer in the midst of hardship. Secondly, he may become a clown, a buffoon, or a jester, thus accepting the stereotype of himself and making

9. Richard Wright, *Native Son* (New York, Harper & Bros., 1940).
10. *Ibid.*, pp. 297–298.
11. *Ibid.*, pp. 330–331.
12. Gallagher states that "a divided society tends to drive its divisive and disintegrating forces into the vital inner processes of personality. The baneful effects are not limited to either caste. . . . It is likely that the victim of persecution is not more seriously warped in personality than are his persecutors. Hatred not only does something to the victim; it also marks those who do the hating." *Op. cit.*, pp. 105–106.

the best of it for his own ends. Again, he may resign himself to the situation "with varying degrees of sullenness or moroseness." Lastly, he may become embued with such resentment that he is bitter and revengeful. Says Gallagher of this type, "Or he may strike out blindly against whatever members of society happen to be nearest and most obviously in his way at a particular time of emotional strain; and the jails have another 'criminal' to whom they may furnish board and lodging." [13]

The various observations reported above are corroborated by findings of experts working on the National Youth Commission. It is pertinent to quote a statement from a report of that group.

More specifically, the research studies have revealed: that being a Negro in most cases not only means living in the presence of severe economic limitations, but, more important for personality development, also means living in an intimate culture whose incentives, rewards, and punishments prevent the development of that type of personal standards, attitudes, and habits, which the general community deem desirable. [14]

Implications for religion in education. The foregoing discussion of the social setting of Negro higher education affords a background for the understanding of the peculiar role which a religious program of the Negro college may need to play in fulfilling its function. We have seen that the American Negro has many inescapable social, economic, and psychological factors in his environment which vitally affect his development of personality and determine his social outlook. In the case of Negro youth of college age these environmental influences often tend to discourage them from striving to reach their highest possibilities.

Religion is life, and the religious program of the Negro college will need above all to be related to the kind of life which its students live. Whatever adequate adjustment a minority group makes to the disadvantages imposed upon it by the majority must be ultimately made in spiritual terms. If it is one of the fundamental tasks of the college to prepare a dynamic leadership for society, it must give heed to meeting as effectively as possible the spiritual needs of the students as well as of the community

---

13. *Ibid.*, pp. 105–106.

14. Quoted in Wright, *op. cit.*, p. x. In commenting on this statement in the Introduction to Wright's novel, Dorothy Canfield Fisher states, "In other words, our American society creates around all youth . . . a continual pressure of suggestion to try to live up to the accepted ideals of the country—such ordinary, traditional, taken-for-granted American ideals as to fight injustice fearlessly; to cringe to no man; to choose one's own life work; to resist with stout-hearted self-respect affronts to decent human dignity, whether one's own or others'; to drive ahead toward honestly earned success, all sails to the old American wind blowing from the Declaration of Independence. But our society puts Negro youth in the situation of the animal in the psychological laboratory in which a neurosis is to be caused, by making it impossible for him to live up to those never-to-be-questioned national ideals, as other young Americans do."

in general. The church is not prepared to undertake sole responsibility for the spiritual ministrations to its constituency. The responsibility of institutions of higher learning in this area is quite real. For these reasons, colleges need increasingly to examine their objectives and programs in order to ascertain in what directions they are moving.

The objectives of higher education among Negroes as stated in college catalogues and in published statements of students of Negro education. In the light of the social setting of Negro education, as well as in the light of the religious background of higher education in America, it is pertinent to examine current statements of the objectives of the Negro college in order to see in what terms their purposes are stated. Obviously, if college administrators do not take cognizance of the peculiar problems presented to them by the society in which Negro education proceeds, there will be a tremendous gap in the higher education of this group.

It can be said at the outset that the implications of the foregoing discussion of the caste status of Negroes suggest that the Negro college, at least from one point of view, has a dual task to perform. In general, the primary task is that of helping students to make the proper adjustment to their society; and, in the second place, the college has the task of providing spiritual resources by means of which adequate adjustment to life is facilitated. Neither one of these purposes can be properly pursued without reference to the other. The stated objectives of Negro education will offer something of a clue to understanding what is being thought and said with respect to these two purposes.

For this study an analysis was made of the catalogues of 42 representative Negro colleges. The catalogues from which the material was gathered were variously for the school years 1938–39 to 1940–41. The *Educational Directory* of the United States Office of Education for 1940 lists 108 Negro institutions of higher education in this country. Taking this as accurate, the catalogue study of objectives embraces approximately 38 per cent of the total number of Negro colleges in America.[15]

According to their catalogues, the total enrollment of the colleges studied was 22,236, or approximately 55 per cent of the total Negro collegiate population.

Included in the study were 17 church-related colleges, 17 public colleges, and 8 private colleges. Of the 17 church-related colleges, 10 were accredited Class A and 7 were accredited Class B. Of the 17 publicly supported colleges, 14 were accredited Class A and 3 Class B. No unaccredited college was included in the study. These 42 colleges may be taken as representative, therefore, of the general trend in higher education among Negroes.

In addition to the catalogue study, an analysis was made of the pub-

15. The list of colleges included in the catalogue study may be found in the Appendix.

lished opinions of twenty representative leaders in, or students of, higher education among Negroes as expressed in books or in periodicals. These statements usually fall within the period from 1926 to 1939, the majority, however, being written in the ten-year period from 1929 to 1939. The attempt is here made to evaluate all these statements of objectives of Negro education in the light of the present status of the Negro and the part which religion may have in the objectives of higher education.

For convenience, the methods used by Koos and Crawford in their study of "College Aims, Past and Present" was followed.[16] These two writers studied statements of college aims by various leaders in higher education and then made a classification of these stated aims for the purpose of comparing past conceptions of objectives (1842–76) with later conceptions (1909–21). In our study we have made a comparison of the Negro college catalogue statements of objectives with the statements of representative students of the problem. At the same time, incidental comparisons were made with Koos's and Crawford's findings for the second period of their study. Attention is called to the probable slight fallacy in this comparison with Koos and Crawford's study in view of the fact that the statements they studied come from a period no later than 1921, while the majority of the statements of the present study come from the decade of the 'thirties. Nevertheless the comparisons will have some value.

The significance of college catalogue statements of objectives. It is not assumed here that the published objectives of the college are in all cases taken seriously by the college in the planning of the curriculum or in its administrative and student programs. They are often printed in the catalogues as a matter of form or of publicity. As Gallagher well says:

The announced objectives of the colleges have been "training for leadership," "training for Christian character," "intellectual growth," and the like; but the testimony of collegiate practice indicated that the real objectives, as distinguished from the catalog pronouncements, have been those of imparting predetermined quantities of subject matter under the threat of examinations with an effort to get a reasonable modicum of memory work on the part of the student and where possible, to add to this the occasional serious attempts to add lessons in morality or to cultivate habits of critical thinking.[17]

We will not be misled, therefore, in assuming that the declared objectives are the real objectives. Our primary interest is in seeing what, in moments of reflection, college administrators have wanted others to regard as their fundamental reasons for existing.

Objectives found. Table V shows the relative percentages of statements favoring various educational goals. It is to be borne in mind that the

16. *School and Society*, XIV (December 3, 1921), 499–509.
17. Gallagher, *op. cit.*, p. 227.

TABLE V

COMPARATIVE ANALYSIS OF STATEMENTS OF OBJECTIVES
OF HIGHER EDUCATION AMONG NEGROES

Statements Calling for Values in	Catalogue Statements Favoring Percentage	Leaders' Statements Favoring Percentage	Statements in Koos and Crawford's Study Percentage
1. Occupational training	59	40	27.5
2. Liberal education	59	15	75.0
3. Morality and character	57	50	62.5
4. Development of scholarly interest and ambition	45	25	27.5
5. Pre-professional training	42	25	32.5
6. Civic and social responsibility	40	45	75.0
7. Training for leadership	33	25	27.5
8. Religious training	30	35	35.0
9. Training for life's needs	28	50	25.0
10. Pre-graduate training	26	5	–
11. Physical efficiency	23	25	7.5
12. Culture	23	20	–
13. Mental discipline	21	25	35.0
14. Philosophy of life	21	30	–
15. Mastery of tool subjects	18	10	–
16. Specific racial needs	14	25	–
17. Unified world view	11	25	–
18. Recreational and aesthetic aspects of life	11	15	20.0
19. Correct use of leisure	11	15	–
20. Understanding current social and economic problems	9	20	–
21. Speech	7	5	5.0
22. Community needs	7	30	–
23. Initiative	7	10	–
24. Guidance and exploration	7	40	17.5
25. Social reconstruction	–	25	–
26. Promoting research and publication	–	10	–
27. Domestic responsibility	–	–	15.0
28. Knowledge for its own sake	–	–	10.0
29. Selection for higher education	–	–	10.0
30. Democratizing college education	–	–	7.5
31. Coördination of student's work	–	–	5.0
32. Attention to individuals	–	–	5.0
33. Opportunities for specialization	–	–	2.5

classification of certain statements was not an easy task, in view of the fact that this writer found, as did Koos and Crawford, that "misrepresentation of an author's meaning is not always avoided, because meanings shade into one another almost imperceptibly and because it is at times impossible to take account of all inter-relationships of purpose expressed or implied." [18]

Objectives found in at least 25 per cent of the catalogue statements examined were in general of the traditional type and corresponded to those found by Koos and Crawford in their study. In the first ten objectives are observed emphases in utilitarian values, the moral and spiritual development of the individual, as well as preparation for study beyond college.

The objectives having the highest percentage of recognition by the colleges were those of *occupational training* and *liberal education*. Fifty-nine per cent of the catalogues studied listed some form of occupational preparation, usually teacher training, as one of the major objectives of the colleges. Less than half of the church-related but more than two thirds of the state colleges listed occupational training as one of their major tasks. At the same time, 40 per cent of the leaders' statements indicated that the Negro college should provide occupational training for its students. In spite of the large number of statements favoring occupational training some objection to it is to be noted. One institution definitely committed itself against it as follows:

The primary object of the college is not *vocational*. It is felt that specialization too often makes adjustment more difficult if not impossible. As in the lower animal kingdom, specialization is definitely related to extinction. While certain courses of a vocational nature are included in the curriculum, they are to be regarded as tools incident to a broader adjustment. The primary aim of the entire educational program is the goal of more efficient social adjustment of the individual in a world of economic and social change.[19]

Incidentally, the Koos and Crawford study showed that not more than 27.5 per cent of the statements they examined favored occupational training as an objective of college education.

It is to be expected that, since the large majority of catalogues studied were those from liberal arts colleges, one of the two most frequently found objectives called for values in *liberal education*. A total of 59 per cent of the colleges refer more or less specifically to this as one of their major aims. Only 3, or 15 per cent, of the published statements of the leaders refer to this objective. Thus, of all the statements canvassed, an average of 43.5 per cent called for values in liberal education. It is sig-

18. *Ibid.*, p. 500.
19. Philander Smith University, *Catalogue*, August, 1939.

nificant, however, that Koos' and Crawford's study showed 75 per cent of the statements called for values in this area. Decreasing emphasis upon liberal education on the part of the writers of published statements may be due to the increased emphasis upon other phases of college aims thought to be more practical.

Although the largest number of catalogue statements referred to occupational training and liberal education as objectives, the aim having the greatest number of references from the point of view of both the catalogue and the leaders' statements was that of *morality and character*. In 57 per cent of the catalogues and 50 per cent of the statements of leaders emphasis was put upon this objective.

Some of the statements were quite emphatic on this point, as, for example:

Attitude toward life is considered of more importance than the mere acquisition of knowledge. . . . Added knowledge should go hand in hand with practical application of knowledge; straight, courageous thinking with honesty, clean living, thorough-going-mastery of the task in hand, kindness and helpfulness to one's neighbors, on the campus and in the community.[20]

This marked emphasis upon morality and character as objectives of college education suggests that, at least from the point of view of published opinions, both college authorities and students of Negro education give highest place to these intangible factors which undergird the successful personality. Because of the poor residential environments from which most Negro students come, the development of moral and spiritual values must inevitably constitute one of the most important ends in education. Here the college may well carry out the fulfillment of certain obligations imposed upon it by the caste society in which it operates. Yet this obligation is considered of importance by all educators regardless of race. Sixty-two and five-tenths per cent of the statements in Koos' and Crawford's study called for values in morality and character, only two other objectives taking precedence over these.

The recognition of *religion* as an aim should be considered here although it ranks ninth on the list of objectives noted. In spite of the fact that the majority of Negro colleges, like most other American institutions, were established by religious forces for religious purposes, in only 30 per cent of the catalogue statements of objectives and in 35 per cent of the leaders' statements was specific reference made to religious training as an educational end. A similar number of statements in Koos' and Crawford's study, 35 per cent, referred to religious training as an objective of college education. From the bare statistics, then, it appears that

20. Spelman College, *Catalogue*, April, 1939.

students of Negro higher education do not place any more emphasis on religion as an objective than students of higher education in general do.

While these statistics are doubtless indicative of the relative amount of interest in religion as an objective many college officials have, they, nevertheless, do not present a complete picture of the situation. In some tax-supported institutions are to be found administrators and teachers who have a real interest in religious values but who do not feel free to emphasize this interest in published statements relative to the purpose and function of the school. As a rule, Negro state colleges give more place to religion in their programs than do white state institutions. This is done all the easier because the Negro student population is usually more homogeneous religiously than the white groups are, particularly more so than white groups in the North. One is inclined to the view, therefore, that the interest of the colleges in religious values as an end in education is perhaps more extensive than the figures suggest. Certainly the values to be found in religion as a factor in personal adjustment are indispensable for higher education. The colleges for Negroes may not wisely neglect emphasis upon these values.

Theoretically, at least, the colleges are interested in the traditional objective of developing *scholarly interest and ambition,* as is shown by the fact that 45 per cent of them included this in their catalogue statements of objectives. This objective ranks fourth on the list as far as the colleges are concerned. Of the writers whose opinions were examined, only 25 per cent referred to this objective. Similarly, 27.5 per cent of the statements in the study of Koos and Crawford called for values in this area.

Ranking fifth and tenth respectively in the list of aims of Negro college education were *pre-professional* and *pre-graduate training.* As many as 42 per cent of the catalogues examined listed pre-professional training as an objective, while 26 per cent emphasized preparation for graduate study. These aims were listed by 25 and 5 per cent of the leaders' statements respectively.

Training for *civic and social responsibility,* for *leadership,* and for *life's needs* were the remaining three objectives listed by at least 25 per cent of the catalogues. Forty per cent of the colleges and 45 per cent of the leaders held that civic and social responsibility should be an aim of Negro higher education. This aim is recognized in such a statement as the following:

It (the college) aims to prepare Negro leaders for wholesome participation in community life. Toward this end, it seeks to make students intelligently sensitive to the problems of life, giving them a foundation in liberal and vocational education that will aid in coping with these problems. The college seeks to emphasize as points of departure, the Negro and Louisiana.[21]

It is significant to note here that, while training in civic and social responsibility ranks sixth in the list of objectives found in Negro college publications, it is one of the two objectives most frequently recognized in the group of statements studied by Koos and Crawford. In this latter study, the objective in question and that of liberal education were each listed in 75 per cent of the statements examined. Also of interest is the fact that a larger percentage of leaders referred to this objective than did college officials in catalogue statements.

Leadership is mentioned slightly less often proportionately by the leaders than by the colleges in their catalogues. In many cases where this was mentioned it was felt that leadership by the college product should be exercised in professional occupations as well as in community and social welfare. Such aims are variously expressed. One college avers that it proposes to "provide a type of education that will contribute economic and social leadership for the group which the college seeks to serve." Another states that it offers, through its college of liberal arts and theological department, "basic training for leadership in the ministry, medicine, law, teaching, social service, and other professions and employments." "To develop intelligent Christian leadership" is another college's way of expressing one of its purposes. In all, 33 per cent of the colleges and 25 per cent of the leaders in education specifically expressed leadership as an objective of higher education among Negroes.

In this study a distinction was made between training for *life's needs* and training for *specific racial needs*. Special attention was given to all the statements to see if the colleges, as institutions of a caste group, as well as the students of Negro education themselves recognized the economic and social situation in which the education of Negroes proceeds. All such statements discovered were, therefore, listed separately from the general statements of preparation for the needs of life. While 28 per cent of the colleges recognized in general the necessity for preparation for life's needs, 50 per cent of the leaders emphasized this objective. Proportionately this latter figure is twice that of the findings of Koos and Crawford. On the other hand, only 6 of the 42 colleges studied made any definite reference to the specific objective of preparation for racial needs, 4 of which were state institutions. One of the most definite statements on this point was the following: "The University proposes to assist its students in meeting, with understanding and decision, the group of acute problems which they currently face by virtue of their racial identity, and in devel-

---

21. Southern University, *Catalogue*, August, 1939.

oping a perspective of race relations in the world.[22] Another college determines, among other things, "To develop in the student an interest in the achievement of the Negro with special emphasis upon the problems of his life in America and his future progress. . . . To aid the student to act intelligently in solving his racial problems." [23]

It is doubtless true that other colleges recognize preparation for racial needs as a distinct objective, even though they make no definite reference to it in their statements of aims.

A much larger percentage of objectives of Negro higher education refer to *health* than Koos and Crawford found in their study. These writers observed 3 instances, 7.5 per cent, where physical efficiency was mentioned as an objective. The present study revealed that 23 per cent of the college statements and 25 per cent of the opinions studied maintained that health education should be one of the specific aims of the Negro college. This difference may be due in part to the recognition by students of Negro education of the unwholesome conditions under which many of the constituency of the Negro colleges live while at home and the consequent necessity on the part of the college to help alleviate this situation.

Of the other aims found in less than 25 per cent of the catalogues studied but which should be considered briefly here are those of the development of a *philosophy of life, guidance,* and *social reconstruction.* Twenty-one per cent of the colleges and 30 per cent of the writers studied felt that the college should help the student to cultivate a philosophy of life. This is closely related to another aim, that of helping the student toward a unified world view, which appears 5 times in each set of statements. A noteworthy emphasis is to be observed on the part of writers in the field of higher education among Negroes upon the necessity for adequate guidance for Negro students. Forty per cent of the opinions studied, as compared with only 7 per cent of the college statements, made specific reference to this objective.

No college in its catalogue statement of objectives referred specifically to the role of the college in social reconstruction, although in one or two cases this may have been implicit in other statements. On the other hand, 25 per cent of the opinions of leaders were more or less emphatic in insisting that this should be one of the purposes of the Negro college. Gallagher's study, to which several references have already been made, is devoted to the exposition of the thesis that the Negro college should have social reconstruction as its main educational task.

Some issues in the determination of higher education among Negroes. In the light of the foregoing study of the announced objectives of higher education among Negroes, it is well at this point to consider more spe-

22. Dillard University, *Catalogue*, 1939, p. 10.
23. Louisville Municipal College, *Catalogue*, 1939, p. 3.

cifically some of the issues involved in determining a philosophy of Negro higher education.

There is no doubt that the most pertinent single factor affecting the education of Negroes in America is the factor of race. Of course it must be readily admitted that race is not the only important factor entering into the situation, for in the final analysis there are the larger problems of human relations which must be considered in any educational scheme. But certainly the most immediate issue for which some adequate solution is necessary is that of the status of the Negro in the American social order. It is from this social situation that many of the serious problems of Negro education in general and Negro higher education in particular derive their origin.

A second issue which serves to determine the objectives of higher education of Negroes is that of the economic status of the group. Some of the patent arguments on this point were examined in the review of the development of Negro education in Chapter I.[24] The issue is still raised from time to time. There is a school of thought that asserts that the Negro must, in the light of his economic and social status, content himself largely with the education of his hands in order to be able to do the laborious work of the world and gradually rise in the scale of economic and social advancement. As we have seen, this was the educational philosophy of Booker T. Washington. Hampton and Tuskegee have been the leading examples of this type of educational philosophy in practice. But even at these schools, in response to popular demands there has been developed a liberal arts curriculum in addition to the regular vocational courses. Some of those who advocate vocational education for the Negro are said to do so in the belief that that kind of education will serve to "keep the Negro in his place." This, however, is not true in all cases but it has been proved to be so in some instances.[25] As far as actual college opinion is concerned, it has already been shown earlier in this chapter that the Negro colleges believe in both types of education for their students, although, in the majority of instances in which the liberal arts colleges gave vocational training as an objective, that training consisted mainly in the preparation of teachers.

Relation of present problems in higher education to Negro education.
A third issue in the problem of higher education for Negroes is the matter of the present status of higher education itself. We have seen how in the past Negro colleges were patterned after the white colleges, and this was to be expected in the light of the background of those who pioneered in Negro education. Higher education in general, however, has been crit-

24. Pp. 12–14 ff.
25. H. M. Bond, *The Education of the Negro in the American Social Order* (New York, Prentice-Hall Co., 1934), pp. 196 ff.

icized more or less severely in some quarters on several grounds. A good summary of these recent criticisms is to be found in Gallagher's study. One quotation will suffice:

A cursory examination of American collegiate practice suggests (a) that the actual practices of typical colleges are such as to deny to the students their rightful opportunities to mature as social beings during their collegiate experiences; (b) that there is a strong tendency of collegiate life to destroy nascent idealism and blunt ethical sensitivity; thus defeating efforts to grow in social-mindedness; and (c) that in the light of the two foregoing deficiencies, looked at from the standpoint of social functioning, the long standing and periodically recurring debate between classical and vocational education is irrelevant and misleading.[26]

Evidence is not lacking that there is justification in altogether too many instances for the criticisms given above. Moreover, the current movement in the reorganization of higher education poses the problem of what should be the relation of educational practices in Negro colleges to the current reorganizational trends. Much discussion has developed in recent years concerning the problem, as is evidenced by the fact that the *Journal of Negro Education* devoted its July, 1936, Yearbook number to the question, "Reorganization and Redirection of Negro Education." It is probable that in the future much will be done in this area.

The "functional Negro college." Earlier in this chapter reference was made to the emphasis appearing in recent years on the part of leaders in Negro education upon the matter of the function of the college in social reconstruction. As has already been indicated, the outstanding extended treatise on the subject is that of Gallagher. Starting with the premise that there should be a sociological approach to educational problems, he concluded that "the educational task is the task of social reconstruction." Gallagher feels that the functional college for Negroes will be aware of the other agencies besides itself which are working in the area alleviating the plight of the Negro and will also "jealously guard itself against all attempts to fix and to crystallize its form, methods, or objectives." [27] Positively, he contends that the functional college should leave the old traditional moorings and launch out upon an "experimentalist and instrumentalist" approach to education. Among other things, this will involve:

(a) Increasing the area of positive knowledge which rests on empirical evidence; (b) cultivating the powers of critical intelligence; (c) overcoming fear which casts its pale shadow across the native hue of resolution; and (d) bringing critical intelligence and social insight to bear upon each other and upon the problem of caste, to the end that social intelli-

26. Gallagher, *op. cit.*, pp. 217–218.
27. *Ibid.*, pp. 248–249.

gence is cultivated in the harmonious interaction and mutual support of social sentiments and critical intelligence.[28]

Besides Gallagher, Du Bois and Bond have given expression to this idea of the peculiar opportunity for social reconstruction which the colleges should have as their *raison d'être*. Quotations from each of these leaders in Negro education are so pertinent here that they should be included at length in this discussion. In his address, "The Field and Function of the Negro College," Du Bois says,

The American Negro problem is and must be the center of the Negro American University. . . . You are teaching American Negroes in 1933, and they are the subjects of a caste system . . . and their life problem is primarily this problem of caste. . . . Unless the American Negro today, led by trained university men of broad vision, sits down to work out . . . exactly how and where he is to earn a living and how he is to establish a reasonable life in the United States or elsewhere, the university has missed its field and function and the American Negro is doomed to be a suppressed and inferior caste in the United States for an incalculable time.[29]

Horace Mann Bond makes the following statement of the social mission of the Negro college in his address, "The Liberal Arts College for Negroes: A Social Force":

. . . the contemporary college needs to have a mission, although it may not have a missionary on the lot. . . . We need to make ourselves conscious of the social forces at work in the world around us, and construct our programs largely in accord with those forces. . . . The contemporary liberal arts college for Negroes needs to align itself with social forces and derive its mission from them, if it is to make a notable contribution. . . . There is nothing mystical in the effect of the sturdy missionary teachers on the Negroes they taught; their impress was revolutionary, but so was their faith and their message. . . . It is my belief that the college of liberal arts for Negroes has, almost ready-made, its imperative mission defined, as a distinctive social force in American life.[30]

Conclusions. In this chapter it has been our purpose to examine two general factors in recognition of which the place of religion in higher education among Negroes must be conceived. In the first place, the societal situation in which Negro education proceeds is one that places a responsibility upon the colleges which is over and above the responsibilities of higher education in general. The caste society of American life inevitably affects the total program of the Negro college, for the youth for

28. *Ibid.*, pp. 249–250.
29. W. E. B. Du Bois, "The Field and Function of the Negro College," *Fisk News*, VI (June, 1933), 1 ff.
30. Quoted by Gallagher, *op. cit.*, p. 250.

whom the college is responsible are the victims of many of the economic and psychological hazards of underprivileged caste status. Secondly, programs and objectives of Negro college, must be envisioned in the light of this fundamental sociological situation. But not the least of the objectives conducive to the alleviation of the difficulties imposed by the social structure are those centering in the development of moral and spiritual perspectives by means of which the individual may not only make a wholesome adjustment to his world but also be stimulated to share in the work of building a better world.

As already observed, there is no doubt that more colleges hold that they have a distinctive task of preparation for racial adjustment than appears in this study. In view of the larger proportion of writers in the field who recognize this problem, it is reasonable to suppose that as colleges revamp their catalogue statements of objectives, more attention will be given to making their statements of purpose specific at this point. Such other purposes as "social reconstruction" and "understanding current social and economic problems" will doubtless receive more attention in the future.

Although the newer emphasis in higher education among Negroes is at the point of the societal factors which play so large a part in the lives of the members of this group, it is never to be forgotten that, in addition to social perspectives, there is needed a spiritual dynamic that will give meaning to the educational process, which will be for each member of or participant in it the ultimate motivation as well as the ultimate end. Organized religious agencies have, historically, attempted to provide this deeper meaning to the business of education. While the development of morality and character ranked third in the list of objectives examined in this study, religious training as a specific objective ranked ninth. Yet it is probable that more college authorities are concerned about religious values in education than the statistics suggest. In any case, the psychological effects of the caste barriers upon the Negro in American society demand, among other things, those spiritual forces which bring about the integration and realization of the self without which life loses its essential meaning. For this reason, the place that is given to religion in higher education among Negroes becomes a matter of no small concern.

III

THE ATTITUDES OF ADMINISTRATORS AND TEACHERS TOWARD THE FUNCTION AND STATUS OF RELIGION IN HIGHER EDUCATION AMONG NEGROES

ONE of the presuppositions of this discussion is that religion, related as it has been to the history and development of higher education and interpreted in terms of a dynamic force for the integration and enrichment of human personality, has a unique role to play in the realization of the total objectives of the college, particularly those objectives leading toward the mastery of handicaps imposed by a caste society. Given the social setting of higher education among Negroes, what can be said to be the place which religion has in the present collegiate training of this group? What attitudes do college presidents themselves have toward the relation of religion to their objectives? What are the college faculty members thinking with reference to the importance of religion to the program of the Negro college? Such questions as these have an important bearing upon the determination of the place which religion holds in higher education among Negroes.

The data for this chapter come partly from personal interviews with 18 presidents of Negro colleges during the school year 1940–41. These presidents, with one exception, were in Class A colleges representative of the highest standards in American Negro education. Of the 18 presidents interviewed, 7 were presidents of state schools, 6 of church-related institutions, and 3 of private schools. In 13 of these colleges, conferences were held with small faculty groups ranging in size from 5 to 25 in attendance. An effort was made in each case to secure teachers from various departments of the college, not simply those interested in religion by virtue of official connection with the campus religious program.

Religion and the public college. The state colleges for Negroes, beginning their development later than the church and private schools, have nevertheless generally outstripped the latter in relative rapidity of growth. Proportionately, they have much more income. They are able to build large plants and to provide generally better physical facilities than the average church-related college. In matters of curriculum, the program of courses offered in the state schools has been constantly increased and enriched, thus presenting one other area of competition to the dominance once enjoyed by the church and private institutions. At this point, the situation in Negro institutions is not very different from that in other colleges. As summed up in a report a few years ago, "There is nothing now singularly different about the church college curriculum, aside from richer offerings in religious subjects." [1]

The problem of the presentation of religion in the Negro church-related and private colleges does not vary appreciably from that in the tax-supported schools, except at the point of legal restrictions which obtain in a few states. In general, the state colleges for Negroes have been able to emphasize religion much more than other state institutions, primarily because of the religious homogeneity of their constituency. Negro students on the whole are Christian and predominantly Protestant, as was brought out in an earlier discussion.[2]

A second factor which has enabled the Negro state college to present much more of a religious program than other state schools is one that is difficult to document but is generally conceded. This is that those who control the distribution of funds to Negro colleges in many cases are inclined to allow greater freedom in religious activities in accordance with the view that religion may be "a good and safe thing" for the Negro to have.

The presidents of three state colleges reported during the interviews that the requirements of state laws made it difficult for them to promote a religious program that measured up fully to their ambitions. On the other hand, two presidents of state colleges reported having no legal difficulties in promoting their religious program. In both of these colleges regular compulsory Sunday school and religious chapel exercises are held. In one of these a regular chaplain and teacher of religious courses was employed. Nine other state colleges reported through the questionnaire study, to be reviewed later, that there were compulsory strictly religious exercises held on their campuses.

Religion and higher education as seen by college administrators. The principal questions raised during the interviews with the college presidents related to the problems students faced during their campus experience, the bearing of religion on the objectives of the college, and the improvement of the religious program of the college.

No college president interviewed expressed any doubt that religion had a fundamental place in the life of the college. Although some were not as expressive as others on this point, there was general agreement that the function of religion in higher education is unique and that it should be one of the objectives of the college to provide as wholesome a religious environment and program as is commensurate with the demands of practicality. These demands of practicality varied with each college situation.

1. Hugh Hartshorne, *et al., Standards and Trends in Religious Education* (New Haven, Yale University Press, 1933), p. 220.
2. Cf. p. 22, Table III.

Said one president of a private college, "Religion is a definite need in the life of the student. Yet it should not be presented in the name of 'Bible-slapping,' long prayers and excess emotionalism, but rather as vitally related to the practical affairs of life. . . . Religion lends essential meaning to education, otherwise education is futile." This president based his assertion on the recognition of two basic aspects of man's life, the economic aspect and the aspect of human brotherhood. In his view the task of the college should embrace the preparation of the student so that he may adequately be able to participate in both of these aspects of life. He also held that religion was the indispensable factor in helping to create societal relations based on the idea of human brotherhood.

Another president of a college asserted that "Religion is a fundamental part of university instruction. In order to present liberal education to the student it is necessary to acquaint him with the fundamentals of religion by expert teachers." This president felt that the university owes instruction in religion both to the student and to his parents, and that, of course, it should be given by a man who is religious.

The president of one state college who reported legal barriers in carrying on a religious program nevertheless expressed a deep concern for the necessity of religious instruction and worship. He has made several attempts to secure a program of religious instruction and work with students through other channels such as denominational or interdenominational agencies, but without success. In lieu of this kind of program, the administration of this college vigorously encourages the students to attend a voluntary Sunday school where Sunday-school teacher's training courses are offered along with others. A Sunday church service of a formal nature is compulsory for students in this college three times a month.

Another state college president based his conviction of the necessity for compulsory religious exercises upon the fact that, in his own words, "Students need guidance." It was his opinion that students did not want to be disciplined about anything and consequently resented compulsory chapel. Nevertheless, he felt that on the campus an attitude of religion that is wholesome and worthwhile should be maintained, that all students should be required to participate in the Sunday religious services, and that underclassmen may profit through the compulsory Sunday school provided for them.

Religion and student problems. With regard to the question of the major problems students have in their college experiences, to which religion may have some relevance, the answers were varied. One of the administrators, president of a church college, was of the opinion that actually the students had no problems which gave them, at least, any real concern. The intellectual adjustment, he felt, was fairly well done in most instances. This president felt that the absence of any students who were "social radicals" on his campus was to be regretted inasmuch as that fact may, though not necessarily, indicate that the college is not fulfilling its task in stirring the students to the recognition of the larger issues of society and thus giving to them better problems with which to be concerned than the petty affairs of campus political and fraternity issues.

Of the several problems to which attention was called, the problem of finance was mentioned most frequently. One college administrator asserted that the struggle of the student to secure his education impairs not only his scholarship but his health as well. Other difficulties mentioned were those of adjustment to the intellectual environment of the college, especially in the area of science and religion; the problem presented by the social distractions offered in the community which compete with the college in its attempt to maintain the interest of the student; and the problem of personal morality which is a hangover from high-school experiences. One of the most significant of the answers to this question of the major problems of students was that given by the president of a state college. This official said that, out of his twenty years of experience, he is convinced that the most serious problem college students face is an "unsatisfied yearning for religion." He felt that the students have a deep-seated but unsatisfied longing for spiritual fulfillment and the "fruits of religion." When asked how the college may meet such a problem, this administrator replied quite frankly that he did not know. He felt certain that under the present program the college did not have "the offerings either formal or informal" to satisfy this yearning. This statement of the problem most serious to the religious life of young people in college deserves major consideration, for it lies at the heart of all efforts on the part of the college to give students that world view by means of which they may make a satisfactory adjustment to life. It was clear in other interviews with both presidents and teachers that the majority of them sense this same serious difficulty which students have.

Other problems outlined by one administrator of a church-related college were, first, the problem of the students' being fitted to do something after leaving college; second, the whole question of sex morality in an age when economic requirements force a delay in marriage; third, the problem of "a living faith, that will give men poise in the midst of chaos"; and fourth, the problem of building an adequate faith in spite of the cynicism which certain faculty members themselves express.

Writing on this question, President B. E. Mays of Morehouse College suggests the following religious needs of Negro students:

1. The need to develop a critical but fair appreciation for the Negro church in particular and for the Church generally.
2. The need to have an intelligent understanding of the Bible and a fair knowledge of the historical development of the Christian religion.

3. There should be courses in religion in the college curriculum.

4. The need for contact with people who demonstrate in their person the fact that religion counts.

5. Negro students need authority and this authority is to be found in religion.

6. Negro students need a faith for their day equivalent to that of their enslaved ancestors.[3]

The improvement of the religious program of the college. During the interviews the college presidents were asked in what ways the presentation of religion to students may be made effective or be improved. In general the answers stressed competent faculty people able to inspire students religiously and morally, the influences of wholesome religious exercises, and course offerings in religion. A three-fold program of religion is envisaged by the administrator of one large university. First, professional training in religion in the graduate school on an interdenominational basis; second, instruction in the history and philosophy of religion in the college of liberal arts; and, third, a dean of the chapel whose function is to keep alive religious worship. This worship, of course, is not to be sectarian. Moreover, attempts should be made also to foster the relation of the student with his own denomination in the city.

According to the president of a state university, one of the primary responsibilities of the college is to "vitalize religion" for its students. "Students," he said, "no longer have fear of hell." New incentives are needed to develop the religious attitude. For him, "religion is not a matter of beliefs" but a matter of concrete challenging activity.

On the point of the attitude which the faculty should take toward the student, the president of a church-related college expressed the conviction that the principle of the sacredness of personality should be fostered. Throughout his administration, he said, his personal attitude was to think of each student as his own child. Whether in actual practice this attitude had led to unwholesome paternalism is difficult to say, nor was there any noticeable indication of just what its effect was during the interviewer's brief stay on that campus.

Most of the presidents said that their first consideration in selecting teachers was their competency in their particular fields. On the whole it appears that no strictly religious considerations entered into the judgment of the qualifications of prospective teachers, yet it is quite probable that in many instances competency in religion may be assumed. One administrator, however, did express the conviction that the ability of the candidate to be a spiritual and moral guide to students definitely influenced his final choice of a teacher.

3. B. E. Mays, "The Religious Life and Needs of Negro College Students," *Journal of Negro Education*, IX (July, 1940), 332–343.

Two presidents suggested the need of tying up the religious as well as the entire college program with the life of the community. Said one, "There is a definite need of orienting all courses in the curriculum to the life of the community." Another employs a full-time "Director of Community Relations" who carries on projects in local churches and is responsible to the "Christian Fellowship Council," a faculty-student campus group.

The above reactions of college presidents to questions about the religious life of the campus have the advantage of not having been thought through and written down in advance for publication. It is reasonable to suppose that the latter procedure may serve to reduce somewhat the weight which may be given to opinions for publication on such a subject. On the other hand, when these questions are compared with published materials by leaders in Negro college education there is a general similarity discernible.

Comparison with a related study. In 1938 a canvass was made of twelve presidents of state colleges for Negroes by the *Sunday School Informer* in order to ascertain whether reports of increasing indifference of youth to the church and to religion were justifiable. Eight presidents of these colleges responded to a questionnaire, two of whom were among those interviewed by the present writer.[4]

In response to the question, "Would you regard a man properly educated and adjusted to the universe who is without spiritual experience and religious expression?," all the presidents answered in the negative. One administrator gave as reasons for his answers the following statements:

(a) A man without spiritual experience is shut out from the sources of growth, enrichment and integration of soul. His soul is without anchorage, guidance or refuge in the time of life's storms.

(b) Such a man is unfit for social leadership since no man can inspire loyalty to life's highest values unless these values find expression in his own life.[5]

The question was raised, "Do you have any severe problems in holding or in building religious interests of the students in your college?" The majority of the administrators felt that there was no serious problem here. As one president of a state college expressed it:

I do not see or feel that we have any serious religious problem at this institution. Our students on the whole respond to religious activities of the campus quite freely and voluntarily. Many of them, as a matter of fact, seem deeply spiritual. I am inclined rather to believe that religious in-

---

4. M. A. Talley, "The Problem of Religion in Negro Colleges in Our Country," *The Sunday School Informer*, V (April, 1938), 6–11.

5. *Ibid.*, p. 11.

terest on the whole is growing. Whether or not our present-day procedure in matters of religion meets the needs and offers solutions to the students' present-day problems is an open question.[6]

Another significant opinion is offered in this connection by the president of a college in the deep South. His assertion was that

We do not have any serious difficulty in holding or building up religious interest here for the following reasons: (1) Most of our students come from communities that afford them a splendid religious heritage; (2) the atmosphere of the college is generally religious, made so by the various organizations that stress religious values, and teachers who exemplify a religious character.[7]

On the other hand, another president felt that the problem in his college was decidedly difficult, expressing the situation as follows:

We do have a very severe problem in holding the religious interest of the students, and I believe that the basic reason is the lack of proper emphasis upon religious education. Our public-supported colleges have not yet provided the type of trained leadership for religious education that they have provided for other education. Many of our public colleges are prohibited from entering too far in this field as they have assumed that it is the responsibility of the church. The church, however, in connection with the Negro state colleges, has undertaken no such responsibility, and in most instances, this work is going neglected. The Negro Land Grant Colleges have some religious program, but for the most part, it is secondary to some teacher and it should be primary to someone.[8]

Other significant observations made through this questionnaire survey indicated that, in the minds of the respondents, students did not leave college agnostics or atheists, in spite of the fact that they became disturbed because of certain scientific courses while going through college.

In summary, the predominant attitude of the presidents of Negro colleges toward the place and function of religion on the campus is characterized by a declared recognition, at least, of the fundamental places which religion has in life. No college president, as far as has been ascertained, seriously questions the value of religion in higher education although there is divergence of opinion with reference to the ways in which religion should be presented to students. In most instances there is an admission that some compulsion is necessary for exposing the student to the benefits of religion.

In view of the universal recognition of the value of religion on the part of college administrators, the questions arises: To what extent is current

6. *Ibid.*, p. 10.
7. *Ibid.*
8. *Ibid.*, p. 7.

administrative policy in these schools commensurate with this expressed appreciation for religion? The answer must be made partly in terms of the extent to which the administrator exerts himself to provide the necessary provisions of staff and facilities for the effective carrying on of religious work among students. Statistics on this will be given later. It may be stated here, however, that as the interviewer made various observations during the two or three days of his visits on each campus there were some instances in which the expressed interest in the value of religion found no counterpart in constructive planning for it. As one president has put it, instead of the religious program of the campus being the primary concern of some one individual on the staff, it is often secondary to some teacher's regular college responsibilities. And, it may be added, usually the teacher is already overloaded with a heavy teaching schedule and other extracurricular responsibilities.

For those who feel that religion has a unique role to play in the higher education of Negroes, however, it is significant that theoretically, or in principle, at least, the average president of the Negro college recognizes the importance of religion and the responsibility of the college for making provisions for it.

The attitude of faculty groups toward religion on the campus. Obviously the role of the teacher in the realization of the objectives of education is one of the highest importance. It was the purpose of the interviews with faculty members in Negro colleges to discover what is the characteristic attitude of Negro college teachers toward the significance of religion in what the college is trying to accomplish. In each case these conferences were arranged through an administrative officer of the college and were held on an informal basis. In addition to meeting with small groups of faculty members, the interviewer availed himself of the opportunity of having personal conferences with individual teachers and staff members in various positions of responsibility. In general, the questions raised with the faculty members had to do with the problems students faced in their college life, particularly on the religious level, the religious attitudes of students, and how the presentation of religion to the students may be improved. Other issues were discussed from time to time, but the above-mentioned ones elicited the most concern and interest.

Problems students face. One of the problems that many faculty members recognized in the lives of students was the problem of finance. It appeared that in most colleges the financial problems of many students were acute. In at least two colleges it was agreed that most students feared the lack of security. This is one basis for deciding another problem students face or the problem of choice of vocation. This problem, however, did not receive as much mention in the various groups as did some other issues. It was to be expected that the problem of personal morality should be mentioned by the faculty groups. This included such areas as the use of alcohol, understanding the way to adjust oneself to relations with the opposite sex, and the problem of delayed marriages.

It was generally recognized that the period of transition from the home environment to that of the college results in many of the serious problems students face. The absence of the old sanctions and discipline of the home environment, the widening of one's contact to include many people with standards of morality and of values different from those which the student knew and respected at home, and the problem of making a wholesome, satisfying adjustment to the scientific method, all were problems that presented serious difficulties to the average Negro college student.

Religious attitudes of students. On the religious side, there was a general consensus that the conservative background from which the average Negro college student comes is responsible for many of the religious difficulties he faces in college. Coming from a background where religion was taken for granted and in which he has been taught to have an "unquestioning faith," the student is often stirred to his emotional depths when the old landmarks of certainty begin to crumble. Occasionally a very popular teacher sneers at religion, thus causing the student to examine, perhaps for the first time in his life, the grounds for his faith.

Moreover, one faculty group at least expressed the idea that students think that the faculty members themselves do not take their own professed religion seriously. For example, it was asserted that in this particular college, where students were compelled to go to chapel, the faculty members themselves, for the most part, did not bother to attend. It was felt that students were thus led to question the sincerity of the policy of the college in requiring them to go to chapel when their own teachers had no apparent interest in it. One other cause of confusion in religion mentioned was the various attitudes toward the Bible taken by the different speakers who come to the campus to present religious addresses. Incidentally, one faculty member himself seemed to be disturbed at this point.

The faculty groups were asked concerning the attitudes which students on their particular campus had toward religion. In most instances they agreed, first of all, that the students in their campus communities were about the same as students anywhere else. Few felt that their group of students were unique in their reaction to religion. On the whole, the observations of the interviewer as he visited the various colleges tended to confirm this assertion.

The transition from the conservative religious background of their home community mentioned above is understood by several faculty groups to condition the religious attitude of many students during their college experience. One teacher expressed his view of the situation as follows: "Students have followed the religion of their home church without thinking about it. Upon coming to college they throw off the religion of habit." It was the opinion of this instructor that fundamentally the religious appreciations of the student remain during his college days essentially what they were at his home church.

In regard to the attitude of students toward religion in general there was common agreement on the part of each group. One group of faculty members said, in effect, that the students on their campus had a fairly normal expression of religion, an expression that was not too far removed from that of adult members of the group in which they lived. In another college the faculty group concluded that the students had a sentimental and emotional attachment to religion upon coming to college, adding that, while the students made the adjustment to new ideas they received in other areas of learning, they nevertheless found it very difficult to make such adjustment in the area of religion.

One significant reaction received from time to time was that the students exhibited a lack of understanding of just what religion really is. It was suggested by some that students tend to confuse religion with the church. In their home background they were not led to understand the meaning of religion in its larger terms.

In regard to the problem of the transition experience, it was felt that in the second year the problem of adjustment in the area of religion was the most crucial one of all. Along this same line another teacher in a different school had noted a definite correlation between the decrease in the noticeable interest of the student in things religious and his advancement in classification.

In regard to the attitude of the students toward the church, a suggestion was made that students have very real and serious problems but do not see how religion can help them. Because of their church background many students do not feel that religion has any practical value. Moreover, it was suggested that because many students felt that something was wrong with the church back home, there is, therefore, something wrong with religion. So, in college, they "take a vacation from religion." On the other hand, it was the opinion of one observer that students, in his experience, tended to make a distinction between the church and religion. He expressed the view that while students were genuinely skeptical of the church they nevertheless still had some respect for religion as such. As an illustration of this attitude, he had several times noted skepticism on the part of students with respect to giving money in church. One student, he said, was heard to remark, "I shan't give my money in church: the preacher doesn't need it!"

In spite of the confusion and skepticism on the part of students which many of the faculty groups said existed, there was one point on which they practically all agreed. In almost every one of the discussions, without suggestion on the part of the interviewer, the groups came to the conclusion that fundamentally students are religious and have an abiding interest in its possibilities for themselves. Over and above their pretended indifference to religion and their failure to *talk* about it as they discuss some other of their interests, it was agreed that, on the whole, religion was deep and intimate in the lives of the students. In one group it was stated, "Students have a deep religious yearning." In another, a state school, "Students are hungry for spiritual guidance."

In some places teachers were found who questioned the significance of the students' attitude toward religion. One said, "It doesn't matter what students think about religion. They are not prepared to think correctly about it." Another questioned whether we have a right to expect very much of value in the students' reaction to religion in the light of the background of conservatism from which the students come. This, however, was not the reaction of a majority in that group and, in the judgment of the interviewer, carried relatively little weight with the others present.

All in all, the conclusion to which the faculty conference groups came was that students are really religious at heart. It is sometimes the desire for popularity that makes them appear to be so indifferent to the claims of religion upon them. Rarely was there an agnostic and hardly ever an atheist to be found among Negro college students.

Improving the presentation of religion. It was thought desirable in these discussions to find out what suggestions faculty members would make with respect to the improvement of the presentation of religion to college students. It is significant that in many cases criticisms were made by the faculty groups regarding the lack of adequate administration support for the carrying on of an effective religious program. The members of a state college group expressed the difficulty of ever being able to do anything very effective in religious provisions in view of the fact that the state, theoretically, has "no concern for the soul of the student."

The two most vigorous criticisms of the lack of administrative support for a religious program on the campus came from faculty members in state colleges. Among other things, it was said that the college makes no real emphasis upon religion as is attested by the facts that the majority of the chapel services were of a nonreligious character, no budgetary provisions were made for effectively carrying on religious activities, no adequate staff of workers in the field of religion was provided, and no courses in religion were made available for the benefit of students. One or two teachers in state schools, however, felt that it was neither desirable nor practicable to offer courses in religion in view of the public support of the school. Here it was felt that the only valid basis of presenting religion was as a matter of ethics. One teacher of biology insisted that there was no place for the discussion of questions regarding the religious implications of some of the conclusions reached in his courses. Several of his colleagues were of a different opinion, however.

It was found that teachers were divided on the question of compulsory chapel. In some cases where the requirements had been modified there were those who expressed dissatisfaction with the attitude behind it. In one instance this was interpreted as a lack of interest in religion on the part of the administration. There were others who felt that the school owed the students the kind of orientation in religion which could only be had through compelling them to attend religious services, just as requirements are made for their being exposed to other phases of the educational program. Still others, however, felt that too much compulsion was not good for students, that it puts the emphasis, in the student's mind at least, upon the compulsion rather than upon the ends sought in the religious exercises. One administrative officer was quoted as saying that "requiring the student to go to chapel does something bad to his character."

On the positive side, a number of definite suggestions were made with reference to the improvement of religion in the colleges. With respect to the responsibilities of the administration, it was generally agreed that, as one teacher expressed it, "the university should formally recognize the place of religion in the world. This would have a concomitant effect upon other aspects of the life of the college." Another expressed the responsibility of the college administration in these words: "Let the students feel that religion is really a fundamental part of their lives." Members of a group in a state college came to the conclusion that the college should make religion a "major activity" on the campus instead of letting the religious life take care of itself or, at best, giving only nominal support to attempts at religious development on the campus. It was felt by members of another group that the program of religion on the college campus should be both "structural and functional"; that is to say, religion should not simply be a "segmentized" aspect of the life either of the college or of the individual. Rather it should be the all-pervading influence in the life of the campus. "Religion is life, not theology." Finally, in this connection, the suggestion was made that the college officials should study the process of religious growth in order more effectively to be able to provide a whole religious program for students.

That opportunities for worship should be provided was agreed upon by all the groups visited. Some teachers admitted the difficulty of providing a program of worship that would be entirely satisfactory to the student body, for one reason because all students do not respond to the same thing in a worship program. Consequently, it was suggested that a variety of religious programs should be made available. These would include occasional services in which there would be no sermon, for it was believed that students appreciated this kind of worship program. The use of services of meditative music or of periods of "quiet time" on the campus was felt to be a profitable practice. The value of group worship was generally recognized, especially in one college where there was no opportunity because of lack of facilities for all the students to come together at one time. It was said that "assemblies would help by establishing a point around which emotion may be organized. Associations would be built up in connection with one place."

With respect to the personnel of the college, faculty members felt in general that the real way for an effective contribution to be made to the religious life of the campus was, as one man put it, "Let the faculty be vital!" The truths of religion are "abstract unless vitalized," said another. Recognition was given to the spiritual relation that should exist between the teacher and the student. If this obtains, the teacher will influence the student sometimes even without knowing it. A personnel worker was of the opinion that the confusion which many students had was due to the lack of personal interest in the student on the part of the teacher. It was stressed in some groups that particularly the person in charge of the religious life of the campus should be of the right personal qualifications, for often the effectiveness of a religious presentation is diminished because of ineffective faculty leadership.

In practically all of the faculty groups there was the opinion that the college should provide courses in religion for the benefit of the students. This idea was based partly on the expressed necessity of cultural training, partly on the conviction that "all good education is religious," and partly on the feeling that the Bible has intrinsic values which the student ought to build into his life. One faculty member suggested even that the college may owe it to the students to provide a Bible in each room after the manner of the Gideon Society. One teacher of English suggested that all majors in literature should be required to take courses in Bible. In general it was felt that the college should see to it that the student leaves the institution with much more of knowledge of religion than he had at the time he entered. General orientation courses in religion were suggested as a means of securing this end. From such course provisions it was felt that the student would be able to build a world view for himself that would serve to stabilize his religious, emotional, and moral life. Finally, it was suggested that the teaching of religion should be "humanized," or, in other words, religious courses should be made so vital and pertinent to the present problems of human life that students will inevitably see in religion its historical and present possibilities for motivating the activities of men.

The final group of suggestions made by the faculty groups have to do with the place of student groups on the campus. "The religious spirit of students should be brought out in desirable channels" was a statement in which the members of one group concurred. It was recognized that the time of many students is quite overcrowded with many different types of extracurricular activities, including activities of Greek letter societies, and because of this many of the students feel that they have no time for activities which may be called religious. But such voluntary groups as small, informal discussion or study clubs were thought to be effective. In one or two colleges the necessity for more effective planning and organization of the work of Student Christian Associations was said to be very much needed.

Conclusions. One of the somewhat surprising results of these meetings with faculty groups was the interest shown by each one in the discussion of these problems. The conferences were planned to last from forty-five minutes to an hour but in most instances they went beyond the allotted time. This in itself is an indication that there is a deep-seated interest in the function of religion in education on the part of a large number of college teachers, despite the fact that there are many who appear to be indifferent to religion just as many students do.[9] It is difficult to generalize from the above report whether these opinions and attitudes of teachers are typical of the Negro college teachers throughout the country, yet the present writer is of the opinion that the indications point to that conclusion.

No claim is made here, however, that this assertion of the interest in religion on the part of the teachers conferred with in this study finds a counterpart or witness in the practical activities of the teachers themselves. Admittedly the only interest verifiable during the relatively short visits on each campus was an academic one. The crucial questions are: Is the interest of the faculty in religion merely academic or is it practical? Does it find concrete expression in their own lives and in their relationships with students? Do they, through precept and example, endeavor to provide an interpretation of religion adequate for the peculiar needs of the underprivileged youth whom they serve? Although the investigator was unable himself to arrive at demonstrable answers to these questions due to the limitations of the study, some significant answers are observable in the opinions of the students themselves concerning the religious sincerity of faculty members. These opinions are discussed in Chapter IX.

One would not deny that there is a significant group among the teachers in Negro colleges who can be justly described as indifferent or, in some

9. Howard Thurman, Dean of the Chapel at Howard University, speaking on the subject of the religious situation in Negro colleges in 1939, stated that the dominant attitude of faculty people toward religion in these colleges is one of indifference due to "religious illiteracy." He ascribed this illiteracy to a "complete lack of knowledge of the content of the Bible itself, the great gap between what the person identifies as religion and what religion really is, and the absence of primary contact with people who themselves are having vital religious experience." Yet one is inclined to have more grounds for optimism on this point than this indictment suggests.

cases, hostile to religion. The hostile ones can be said to be a very small minority. In this connection, the results of an interview with Dr. W. E. B. Du Bois, one of the outstanding Negroes in America, is particularly apropos. Dr. Du Bois represents one of the keenest minds of his generation. In answer to the question of what is the place of the Christian religion in the program of higher education among Negroes, Dr. Du Bois replied that in his opinion there was no place whatever for it. It was his opinion that the teachings of Jesus do not influence the education in the colleges today. There is no place in college education for the religion of Jesus which, in his opinion, is to be identified with extreme pacifism, the exaltation of poverty, and the negation of this world in the interest of some future life apart from this world. For him this is essentially what the Christian religion is. It is also a doctrine of "peace at any price." Dr. Du Bois stated in effect that the teachings of Jesus with reference to the love of God and of one's neighbor as himself are not a part of college education. This is not the business of the college. No college student knows or cares anything about them. Dr. Du Bois further contended that organized Christianity represents the wealthy people and their interests primarily. Among the less privileged people, organized Christianity represents the interests of the more well-to-do of these groups.

It is clear to the student of the religion of Jesus that Dr. Du Bois makes the mistake of interpreting it too narrowly. To equate that religion exclusively with pacifism and world denial is not true to the facts. To suggest, as he does, that the death of Jesus represents extreme appeasement of the "powers that be" rather than a positive demonstration of a superior philosophy and method of life is illogical when Jesus' death is seen in the light of the entire body of his teachings.

It is probable that Dr. Du Bois' sensitive nature has been so harassed by the inconsistencies of historical Christianity that he cannot see clearly the positive influences which the religion of Jesus has had upon western civilization. One is inclined to believe that his unusually scintillating insight is not as keen on this point as, given a little more objectivity, it might otherwise be.

As has been mentioned above, if on the whole the faculty members and college administrators accept in principle the position that religion is a *sine qua non* of education, then there is much more hope for the inclusion of religious principles in the educational programs of Negro youth. When these principles are omitted in the attempt to bring members of an underprivileged caste to the abundant life, the outlook for the future adjustment of this group cannot be very bright.

IV

ADMINISTRATION-SPONSORED RELIGIOUS PROGRAMS

AMONG the common criteria for judging whether religion is finding expression in the life of a college are those of public religious exercises and the provision of other facilities by means of which spiritual values find overt recognition. In the institutions of an underprivileged minority these exercises will not be singularly different from those in other colleges. What may be and often are different are the particular emphasis in religion and the points of view which are given to the economically and socially disinherited. In either case, religion can hardly become functional with respect to the total life of the institution unless steps are taken to insure opportunities for both teachers and students, in the words of W. E. Hocking, to "listen to the silent speech of the infinite and the eternal." [1] We are not misled, however, by the erroneous assumption that the mere fact of a chapel exercise or other religious activity on the campus is an indication of the presence of real religion. An administration-sponsored religious exercise may not always be prompted by nor result in a pervading religion, but a pervading religion will almost always result in some opportunity for the corporate recognition of spiritual values.

Having seen, therefore, the attitudes of college administrators and faculty members toward the function and status of religion in higher education among Negroes, it is well to inquire to what extent an admitted interest in religion is finding expression in concrete provisions for it.

Compulsory chapel exercises.[2] The problem of college chapel exercises has often been one of the focal points around which many of the difficulties associated with religion in higher education have centered. The oldest American college was the first to abolish required chapel attendance. After Harvard set this precedent in 1885, gradually other colleges began to modify their requirements of attendance at religious exercises. The issue is yet a live one today, for the majority of the churches and

1. W. E. Hocking, "Can Values Be Taught?" *Obligations of the Universities to the Social Order* (New York, New York University Press, 1933), p. 350.
2. In this and the following chapters the author makes use of statistics gathered by means of a questionnaire designed to show the data regarding the religious provisions to be found in the colleges of the study. Statistics for this chapter come from a total of 44 institutions, of which 19 were church-related, 4 were private, and 21 were supported by public funds. Twenty-five of the schools were accredited Class A, while 19 were either Class B or unaccredited.

private colleges, as well as many of the public institutions, still require attendance at services of a religious nature, even though only once a week.

A review of the extent and nature of the various types of chapel exercises held on the campuses of the colleges of this study leads to the conclusion that the great majority of colleges for Negroes have compulsory chapel services of some kind. Fully 86 per cent of the 44 colleges require attendance at some form of chapel program. The proportions of public and other institutions requiring compulsory chapel attendance are about the same. Since the majority of the institutions not included in this study were small denominational and private schools, it is quite likely that if a study were made of the entire number of Negro colleges, the percentage of those having compulsory chapel attendance would be even larger. This prevalence of compulsory chapel services in Negro colleges may be partly due to the type of constituency from which the students are drawn. As was indicated in Chapter I, the students are largely Protestant in background, and much of the religious heritage is of the traditional other-worldly type. College administrators are, therefore, slow to make modifications in the requirements of attendance at religious services.

Responsibility for planning compulsory chapel. Prior to a few years ago, it was common for the president of the Negro college to assume chief responsibility for the chapel services. While in some instances that situation still obtains, the trend in the more important institutions has definitely been away from this practice. More and more the responsibility has been shifted to other members of the staff or to committees. In 63 per cent of the colleges having required attendance at chapel, responsibility for planning the services rested upon a committee. Some of these were made up of faculty members alone while others were composed jointly of faculty and students. The fact of student participation in the planning of compulsory chapel was made more specific in replies to a definite question on this. The large majority of schools reported that students did have some share in planning the exercises. Nevertheless, 18 per cent definitely indicated that students had no share in this responsibility. But, in view of the fact that only six colleges reported chapel committees made up jointly of students and faculty, it is apparent that in the colleges as a whole much of the student participation in planning the exercises is merely incidental.

The trend toward student participation on faculty chapel planning committees has much significance for the development of student interest and initiative with respect to the exercises they are required to attend. In one instance familiar to the investigator, student reaction against compulsory chapel tended to be somewhat pronounced until the number of services held each week was reduced from five to three and students were given an opportunity to plan as well as to conduct approximately half of the exercises during the school year.

Source of chapel speakers. In the colleges reporting in this study, the majority of chapel speakers were faculty members, as may be expected. Some colleges indicated that as many as 80 or 90 per cent of the chapel speakers were from the faculty. Yet the figures show that, for the 36 colleges giving information on this item, an average of 21 per cent of the speakers were from the student body, with a slightly larger number of state colleges providing this opportunity for students than church-related institutions. In the development of techniques and experience in speaking to large and often critical groups, as well as in helping to build those personal resources for meeting life situations, student participation in chapel programs should be of inestimable value. Certainly the college chapel provides a place where enterprising students may develop powers of leadership, religious, moral, and civic, which they will need upon settling down in any community.

In view of the expressed interest shown by college students in getting the opportunity to hear a variety of speakers, colleges do well to bring in out-of-town persons who have contributions to make to the campus community. Slightly more than 17 per cent of the chapel speakers in the 35 colleges reporting on this item were in this category. Many colleges are handicapped in this regard by lack of funds. The fact that the Class A colleges show a larger percentage of out-of-town speakers than do the other institutions is partly explained by the relatively greater financial resources which the former possess.

Voluntary chapel exercises. It is only in relatively recent years that the colleges for Negroes have begun experiments with voluntary chapel exercises, and this accounts for the relatively smaller percentage of this type of chapel as compared with compulsory services. Yet there are a few colleges in which voluntary chapel programs are the only type held on the campus. For the past ten or twelve years experiments have been carried on in this area and it is quite likely that this trend will continue. It is doubtless true at the present time that most of the voluntary chapel programs held on the campuses of Negro colleges are sponsored by student organizations such as the Christian Association. Here is often afforded an opportunity for students themselves to lead or direct the service.

It is the common assumption that unless chapel services are made compulsory students will not attend. This assumption is supported by the various experiences of persons working in the field of religion in the colleges. College presidents themselves are generally agreed that if the religious or other services are made voluntary students will not attend in any appreciable number. There are some instances, however, of excellent attendance at voluntary religious exercises, but these are the exception rather than the rule.

Yet students themselves assert in surprising numbers that they would attend the chapel services on their campuses if these were made voluntary. In spite of this, one is inclined to the view of the college presidents interviewed in this study; that is, that unless attendance at the chapel services is made compulsory it is likely that not more than 50 per cent of the students will attend regularly.

Certain factors are to be kept in mind, however, when the attempt is being made to estimate the possibilities involved here. Some college campuses are situated in areas somewhat removed from urban or municipal centers. In these instances it is much easier to interest students in programs on the campus, for these offer some opportunity for social contact and recreation that might otherwise be obtained in the urban and municipal centers which constantly offer competing attractions to students. In such types of institutions also, the large majority of the students usually live on the campus. Here it is always convenient to arrange and to receive support for various types of projects involving group participation.

Religious elements in chapel services. A distinction is to be made between the religious chapel service and the student assembly. Between these two types is a third, a combination of the two, or "semireligious" service. The majority of Negro colleges regularly sponsor chapel services of a strictly religious nature, and in most of these instances attendance is required. These services are not all confined to the church-related or private colleges, for almost as large a proportion of public colleges report such services as do other institutions. The semireligious chapel programs are sometimes primarily religious with some nondevotional elements such as speeches on subjects of general interest including economics and social problems and programs offered by fraternity and sorority groups. Other semireligious programs are primarily assembly periods with some religious items used at the beginning. Speakers on current topics, forums, student activity programs, and talks by faculty members are among the various items used in these services. Again, a fairly large proportion of colleges have programs that are classed by them as assembly periods, in which dramatic activities, debates, music programs, as well as speakers on topics of current interest are presented. Yet even here in a few colleges such programs are opened with a hymn and a prayer.

The significance of chapel programs. It is clear from our investigation that the colleges for Negroes attempt to provide opportunities for the religious development of their students through chapel exercises, compulsory or voluntary or both. Although a few colleges report no chapel services of a strictly religious nature, on the whole the opportunities for worship are not neglected by the colleges and it is apparent that chapel programs are relied upon as one of the principal agencies for mediating religion and religious ideals to students. Even in those institutions where there are no strictly religious services, there are, for the most part, chapel exercises of a semireligious nature. Taken as a whole, however, the predominating elements in the chapel programs are religious, although it is difficult adequately to evaluate how effective for the religious life and development of students these services are. Obviously this depends upon the spirit in which the college administers the chapel programs, the extent of student interest and participation, as well as the important question of whether the type of religious thoughts and ideals presented to students is commensurate with their growing intellectual and social development. It should also be pointed out here that chapel programs of a religious nature should afford an excellent opportunity to colleges for breaking down many of the psychological as well as intellectual difficulties imposed by the caste system upon Negro youth. The opportunity to hear outstanding leaders of their own race as well as sympathetic personages of the dominant group have immeasurable values for the student. In addition to this the presentation of religion as a vital factor in individual and social life should make it possible for the growing individual to lay firmer hold upon spiritual values to be incorporated in his own life.

College students themselves are not always able to judge adequately the value of chapel programs as well as other services or experiences which colleges may afford. There are notable instances of alumni whose recognition of the value of compulsory chapel programs became increasingly clear with the passing years and consequent maturity. The students' present estimate of the chapel services will be discussed in a later chapter.

Special occasions for religious emphasis. In the early days of the development of Negro education it was common for the schools regularly to sponsor revival services in much the same fashion as the churches. Often a special evangelist was brought in for the occasion. Within recent years this practice has become refined, although some of the schools still carry on the early traditions in the customary manner. In the majority of the better colleges, the term "revival" has been largely replaced by such expressions as "Week of Prayer," "Religious Emphasis Week," or some designations more commensurate with current trends. It is safe to say that more than three fourths of the colleges for Negroes observe such a period of special emphasis upon religion, usually in the period preceding the Easter season.

There is little difference between the expressed purposes of the Week of Prayer in church-related colleges and those in the public institutions. In general, the objective is that of making religion vital in the lives of the students. One church-related college was said to have as its major objective for the Week of Prayer, "To pray for the students and especially the college." Among other statements of purposes are the following: "To stimulate the Christian students and to inspire others to become Christians."

"To instruct students in the fundamentals of the Christian faith and to have them dedicate or re-dedicate their lives to Christianity." "Spiritual Revivication." "To awaken the students' sense of responsibility to each other and to God." "To give the students some idea of the importance of religion and to aid in the problem of science and religion." By far the largest percentage of speakers for these occasions are brought in from out of town, and the financial responsibility is usually borne by the college administrations, although in a few instances the expense is borne jointly by the administration and student organizations such as the Christian Associations or by the Christian Associations alone. At one church-related college a plan is in operation whereby several outside religious leaders are brought to the campus to spend at least a week in working with students. These speakers are designated "college preachers." This plan is thought to be an improvement over the usual system of having religious emphasis for only one week during the school year. Incidentally, a decreasing emphasis is to be observed in the matter of securing "conversions" during the Week of Prayer among those students who do not profess religion.

Prayer meeting. Prayer meetings on a voluntary basis have long characterized the history of higher education in America. The early history of education among Negroes in America shows also that the colleges quite naturally adopted the prevailing church custom of regular prayer meetings. Today, however, the colleges have gradually moved away from the practice although it appears that the move is not quite as rapid as one might be led to suppose. Evidence of this is that 18, or 41 per cent, of the colleges of this study report that prayer meetings are regularly held on their campuses, and in 8 of these attendance is said to be compulsory. Moreover, 3 of these latter are state schools. In the 10 colleges reporting voluntary attendance at prayer meetings, the estimated average attendance is 89 students per school. If these estimates are anywhere near the real situation, the evidence is conclusive that students have a real interest in religion. One is inclined, however, to the view that if accurate figures for these 10 colleges were available, this percentage would be somewhat smaller.

Sunday-school exercises. One of the significant facts concerning religion in the colleges for Negroes is that most of them sponsor Sunday-school exercises. On the basis of present information, the conclusion is that the proportion of colleges among Negroes sponsoring Sunday-school exercises is perhaps much greater than comparable studies in white colleges would indicate. Thirty, or 68 per cent, of the 44 colleges have regular Sunday schools. Of added significance is that Sunday-school exercises in almost half of the colleges reporting them are compulsory. Seven state-supported institutions report compulsory Sunday-school exercises.

The president of one state college reports that it is impressed upon students that their opportunities for securing good teaching positions are enhanced if, in recommending them, he can say that in addition to the regular courses in the curriculum the students have also taken the courses in religious training. This is one of the factors motivating some students taking the courses, although many undoubtedly take them because they are prescribed. It is well to observe that courses in Sunday-school teacher training are offered in a number of the colleges.

In view of the prevalence of Sunday schools in more than two thirds of the colleges included in this study, it is reasonable to suppose that many of the other colleges not studied also sponsor such features. In this way an attempt is made to provide some of the religious atmosphere in the college which the student had in his home background.

Faculty-student coöperation in religious programs. In the previous discussion on chapel planning responsibility, it was brought out that only 6 colleges reported regular faculty-student committees for this work. Yet it appears that there are indications of a general improvement in the matter of faculty-student coöperation in promoting religious programs. Fifteen, or 44 per cent, of the 34 colleges reporting on this question indicated having a faculty-student committee for planning some or all of the programs. Some form of coöperation involving certain religious organizations of students such as the Christian Associations were operative in 10 of the colleges. Only 3 of the 34 colleges replied that there was no faculty-student coöperation in the planning of the religious life of the campus.

That the above situation represents an improvement is suggested by a comparison with a previous study. In 1929 Mays made a study of the religious attitudes of 400 Negro students located in 8 representative colleges. He found that there was almost no coöperation between the students and faculty in the development of religious programs on the campus.[3]

Counseling provisions for students. In connection with the consideration of religious provisions for students by college administrations it is appropriate to see in what ways colleges seek to meet the need for providing adequate religious counseling for their students. This problem is receiving attention on the part of all those vitally concerned with the programs and objectives of education. This is especially true in higher education in which administrators and personnel officers are endeavoring more and more to develop adequate techniques and facilities for this important enterprise.

As was brought out in Chapter II, the personality problems of Negro

3. Report of the Conference of College Religious Workers, Fisk University, Nashville, Tennessee, March 7–10, 1929, p. 7.

youth are made acute by virtue of the social situation in which the education of this group is carried on. This means that, in addition to the general problems common to all adolescents, Negro youth are the victims of social tensions for which an adequate solution must be found if the student is to make satisfactory adjustment to his world. The religious and moral problems of Negro youth, however, will be generally and in essence the problems which the youth of all groups face.

In order to find out to what extent the colleges are making provisions for this need of counseling, the question was asked, "What provisions are made for counseling students in religious and moral problems?" The largest percentage of replies refer to the director of religious activities or to conferences with religious instructors. Only a few colleges make reference to a specific program of guidance. It is seen also that several of the colleges rely upon the work of the students' religious organizations for counseling provisions. That this is sometimes effective is indicated by the fact that in the questionnaires filled out by students many of them referred to the religious organizations as a source of help in meeting religious and moral problems. In a few instances the annual Week of Prayer is thought of as a provision for religious and moral counseling, an agency, incidentally, that was also attested to by a few students as being of benefit to them in the solution of their problems. Yet one is inclined to question too great reliance upon student organizations, chapel services, or a few days of special religious emphasis each school year for the year-round need of student guidance and counseling on religious and moral problems.

Conclusions. The fact of student participation in planning as well as in executing the religious exercises of the campus should have some bearing on the students' reaction to the religious program of the college. It should mean that the particular kind of religious activity which students appreciate most should be certainly included, and therefore dissatisfaction with compulsory attendance should be reduced considerably. Students, however, generally have little opportunity in determining whether or not the chapel exercise itself is to be compulsory, and hence the attitude of the student body as a whole toward this aspect of the campus religious life may reflect their reaction toward the fact of compulsion rather than their attitude toward the quality and effectiveness of the services. As will be noted later, students offered fewer criticisms of the chapel exercises which were voluntary than of those which were compulsory. In an effort to widen the scope of democratic education, some colleges have a general policy of including students on practically all committees of the colleges. In so far as this practice is thoroughly democratic as regards first the selection or appointment of the students to serve on these committees and secondly the weight which the faculty give to student opinions on the issues involved, it should be in harmony with sound educational and religious principles and should serve as an important factor in the total adjustment which the student makes to his life in general.

The colleges of this study indicated a variety of counseling provisions for students, chief among which were the directors of religious life, faculty members, personnel deans, and instructors in religion. Because only five colleges reported having an advisory system, we may conclude that there is much work that needs to be done along this line among the institutions of this study.

In the dual task imposed upon the Negro college, of bridging the barriers of caste and providing adequate personal resources of the spirit by means of which the individual masters life, the role of the various administration-sponsored religious exercises and facilities is of inestimable possibilities. Through these resources the college may at once provide wholesome interracial contacts which will lay the foundations for mutual understanding and appreciation based upon spiritual values and, in addition, guide the student through coöperative and creative sharing in the religious quest toward the most adequate resources for personal living.

V

THE STATUS OF RELIGIOUS WORKERS

IT is generally recognized as axiomatic that upon the teacher rests the ultimate responsibility for the inculcation of the objectives of the school in the life of the student. This is strikingly true in the case of religious education, where the character of the teacher often proves to be of much more value in determining the religious development of the student than the particular materials which he teaches. The college that attempts to give its students an education that is essentially true to the best there is in the religious tradition will need to employ many forces to obtain this objective, and by no means the least of these influences will be the teachers themselves.

Yet it will not always be the teachers of distinctly religious subjects who will play the most significant role in determining the religious development of the student in college. The teacher of courses in other departments of the humanities, in the sciences, and in the arts will often be even more significant to some students religiously than those in Bible or some other branch of religious study.

In spite of this fact, it is generally held to be desirable and even necessary for the college to pay especial attention to the provision of professional workers and teachers in religion if it is to recognize the essential role which religion has in the life of the individual and in the life of society. For some colleges with limited means this is sometimes difficult in view of the fact that all colleges are faced with the necessity of providing the minimum curriculum required by the standardizing agencies if they are to receive any recognition for their academic work. These minimum curricula do not include work in religion.

A study of the extent to which colleges provide professional workers in religion will reveal, among other things, something of the importance which administrators attach to the significance of religion. As has already been suggested, however, the real importance which religion holds in the mind of a college administrator cannot always be measured in quantitative terms; yet statistics on various provisions for religion on the campus will be helpful.[1]

Directors of religious life. Among the more important ways in which religion may be made effective in the life of the college is through the em-

---

1. The data for this part of the investigation came from 44 institutions, of which 19 were church related, 4 were private, and 21 were public. Twenty-seven, or 61 per cent, of these were accredited Class A.

ployment of personnel upon whom will rest specific responsibilities for the development of religious programs on the campus. There is often the danger here that in placing upon one individual the responsibility of directing the religious life of the campus many people in the college community, both teachers and students, will make the mistake of assuming that only from this member of the staff is one to expect stimulus or guidance for the religious life of the campus community. Be that as it may, the colleges of this study have generally given recognition to the value of placing such responsibility upon one individual. In answer to the question, "Does the college employ a Chaplain, College Pastor, Director of Religious Activities, or any such officer?" three fourths of the colleges replied in the affirmative. These included all except 1 of the church-related institutions, the 4 private colleges, and 6 of the 21 public colleges. While as many as 14 different titles were used by the 33 schools in the designation of this office, there was a strong preference in all types of schools for the title "Chaplain," with the titles "College Pastor" or "College Minister" next in order, followed by the term "Director of Religious Activities."

Of the variety of responsibilities which directors of religious life have, that of teaching courses in religious subjects predominates, as would be expected. The statistics show that 18, or 55 per cent, of the directors of religious life have teaching responsibility in this field. Ten others have teaching responsibility in the field of philosophy and 8 teach in other fields. Four of these officers are deans of the school of religion connected with the college or university where they are employed. Four combine their work with the responsibility of being dean of men. Directing the chapel programs, serving as chairmen or members of committees of religious life and activities, and supervising religious organizations constitute much of the responsibility of a large number of faculty workers in religion.

Age. According to the figures obtained from 24 of the 33 colleges, the men who have the responsibility of the religious programs of the campus are relatively well experienced as far as their chronological ages are concerned. The average age of these workers is 39.3 years, with the admitted range from 29 to 57 years.

Academic rank. Standardized procedures in the academic ranking of teachers have not yet been adopted in the majority of Negro colleges. In some schools this is not even attempted and all teachers, regardless of experience, preparation, productivity, or salary, are considered professors. One of the reasons for this is the relatively small staffs characteristic of most Negro institutions. With this in mind, it was noted that in the 30 colleges which supplied data on this point the majority of religious directors ranked relatively high academically. One third of these workers were listed as having the rank of professor and 7, or 23 per cent, as having the rank of associate professor. Stated another way, 17, or 52 per cent, of the 33 religious directors were either associate or full professors. The proportion of high-ranking men was larger in the church-related colleges than in the public institutions.

Academic preparation. Information on the academic preparation of directors of religious life will at once indicate the progress in Negro education at this point and also will show to some extent the qualifications of these workers for their tasks. It has not been very long since the average Negro college depended for its teachers largely upon men and women just out of college. Within the last 15 or 20 years advance at this point has been quite accelerated, due in large measure to the rise of the accreditation movement. It is therefore significant that the 33 directors of religious life held a total of 77 earned degrees, an average of 2.2 degrees each. Twenty-nine of these degrees indicated some form of specialization in religious study and some of the M.A. degrees were doubtless also in this field.

The highest earned degrees of the directors of religious life ranged from the B.A. to the Ph.D., with noticeable difference in the standards for the Class A schools as compared with the other colleges. The highest earned degrees of 29, or 86 per cent, of the men were above that of the B.A. Although there were other teachers in the field of religion holding the doctorate in religious study, only one director of religious life with this degree was reported among the men of this study. In a later discussion comparison will be drawn between the present study of the academic preparation of religious directors and teachers in Negro colleges and the results of a national survey of this problem.[2]

Other instructors in the field of religion. Sixteen colleges reported 31 instructors other than the director of religious activities offering courses in the field of religion. In 2 instances these were colleges in which the director of religious activities had no teaching responsibilities. These teachers for the most part ranked relatively high academically. Thirteen, or 42 per cent, of them held the rank of professor, 2 were academic deans, 1 was the college president himself, and 1 was an associate professor.

It is significant that the largest percentage of these men have specialized in religious courses. Twenty-two, or 71 per cent, of these teachers' major field of professional preparation was in religious subjects, with religious education constituting the principal area of specialization.

The 31 teachers rank no lower in academic preparation than do the directors of religious life. A total of 70 degrees was earned by the former. Seven, or 23 per cent, held doctorate degrees, of which 5 were the Doctor of Philosophy, 1 the Doctor of Education, and 1 the Doctor of Biblical Liter-

2. Cf. p. 72.

ature. Seventeen, or 55 per cent, held the degree of Master of Arts, while 16, or 52 per cent, held the Bachelor of Divinity degree or its equivalent. Three held the degree of Master of Sacred Theology. It is clear that 23, or 33 per cent, of the 70 earned degrees were taken in various religious subjects, and doubtless some of the 17 Master of Arts degrees were also in this field.

It will be significant to compare the academic preparation of the various teachers of religion with that of the directors of religious life in Negro colleges and also to compare the data on all Negro teachers of this study with statistics for the nation as a whole. In no case does the highest earned degree of various teachers in the field of religion represent less than the Master of Arts, and a much larger number of these have earned the doctorate.

In 1936 Wickey and Eckhart [3] made a study of the academic preparation of teachers of religion in American colleges. When the findings of the present study are compared with those of the national survey some notable results appear. The percentage of teachers with only the college bachelor's degrees is approximately the same in both studies except in the Roman Catholic colleges, as is shown in Table VI. While the Wickey

TABLE VI

COMPARISON OF PROPORTION OF HIGHEST EARNED DEGREES *

Type of Institutions	Number of Teachers	Percentage in the Degree Groups †			
		I	II	III	IV
Private	39	5.1	41.1	5.1	48.7
Roman Catholic	171	11.1	46.2	.6	42.1
Protestant	406	5.2	51.0	6.9	36.9
Negro Institutions	64	4.7	70.3	12.5	12.5

* Adaptation of Table VII from Gould Wickey and Ruth A. Eckhart, "A National Survey of Courses in Bible and Religion in American Colleges and Universities," *Christian Education*, XX (October, 1936), 21.

† Group I includes the college bachelor's degrees; group II, the A.M., B.D., B.Th., and S.T.B.; group III, the S.T.M.; and group IV, the various doctorates.

and Eckhart study shows between 41.1 and 51.0 per cent of the teachers of religion with the M.A., B.D., B.Th., and S.T.B. degrees, 70.3 per cent of the Negro teachers were in this group. The most significant point in the comparison is that only 12.5 per cent of the Negro teachers held doc-

3. Gould Wickey and Ruth A. Eckhart, "A National Survey of Courses in Bible and Religion in American Colleges and Universities," *Christian Education*, XX (October, 1936), 9–45.

torate degrees, while between 36.9 and 48.7 per cent of the teachers in the national survey held doctorates. Of course one would not expect the teachers in Negro colleges to rank as high academically at this stage of Negro education as other teachers do. All things considered, the Negro teachers are not as far behind in this respect as some might suppose. The conclusions to which Wickey and Eckhart came as a result of their findings are in part applicable to the situation among teachers in the colleges for Negroes.

This situation is most encouraging. Teachers of religion have a scholastic training equal to that of the teachers in the other college departments. And their scholastic status is improving. In a study of this subject ten years ago, out of 113 full-time teachers only 30% had the earned doctorate. Today the average is about 40%. Teachers of religion are no longer merely pulpit orators and successful ministers; they are scholars in their own fields.[4]

Comparison with the general status of Negro teachers. This brings us to a consideration of the present status of Negro teachers in general on the college level, which should be an index of what may be expected of the ability of the colleges to carry out the program of social reconstruction which we have seen to be one of its main functions.

In 1931 Knox [5] found that, measured by the requirements of the standardizing agencies, the teachers in the 32 Negro colleges of his study were quite inadequately prepared on the whole. "Not all the professors had earned the A.B. degree; less than fifty per cent had received the A.M. degree, and less than one per cent had received the degree of doctor of philosophy." Since that time, however, the situation has been considerably improved. Marks [6] made a study of the 18 Class A and 18 Class B Negro colleges in 1938. His report shows that 75, or 6.9 per cent, of the 1,085 teachers in Negro schools held the Ph.D. degree or its equivalent. There were 13 of the 36 schools, however, which reported no teachers with the Ph.D. degree. In addition, there were 51 teachers who had no degree at all, while 263 teachers held only the bachelor's degree. Although, as Marks points out, most of the teachers holding no degree at all were in such vocational fields as agriculture and home economics, there were many teaching in such other fields as "English, education, and psychology, etc., where advanced training is certainly to be considered desirable for persons giving instruction at a college level."

4. *Ibid.*, p. 21.

5. Ellis O. Knox, "The Trend of Progress in the Light of New Educational Concepts in a Group of American Colleges dominated by Religious Influences" (Ph.D. dissertation, University of Southern California, Los Angeles, 1931).

6. E. S. Marks, "The Negro College," *Journal of Educational Sociology*, XII (January, 1939), 288–297.

It is apparent that the majority of the teachers in Negro colleges had their graduate training at high-ranking graduate schools. At least 55.8 per cent, says Marks, did their graduate work "at schools of first rank." Another 20 per cent did their work at schools not quite so prominent but which, nevertheless, are institutions recognized as fully equipped to give adequate training in graduate work. At the present time, the improvement of Negro teachers in the colleges along the line of graduate training is moving along at an encouraging rate.

The selection of teaching personnel. A parent and student of education once said, ". . . I am personally more concerned about *who* teaches my son and what happens to *him* in the process than whether he studies 'Greek or gadgets.' " [7] The importance of the well-balanced teacher for the educational process has long been recognized. There are few students of education who still hold narrowly to the "Mark Hopkins and student on a log" idea of education but there is fairly general agreement that without certain qualifications such as attractive personality, adequate training, and sound life philosophy, much of the time spent in teacher-student relationship will be lost.

The Negro college which endeavors to carry out a functional philosophy of education will, therefore, endeavor to include persons on its staff who, first of all, will be vitally concerned with the ultimate purpose of the college and fully devoted to the achieving of its end. While sound scholarship will always be an indispensable prerequisite for the teacher, this qualification will by no means be the sole criterion of judgment. The ideal teacher will be one able and willing to contribute to the development of the entire life of the school. Since educational objectives are not always static, the teacher will be prepared to contribute creatively and constructively to the formulation of new goals for the educational task.

The effective teacher in the Negro college will also be able to help students to discover ways of solving the race problem along sound constructive lines. He will need to be in a position to engender self- and racial respect on the part of Negro students most of whom come from an environment in which they have been altogether too often told that they are inferior. This will involve, among other things, the ability to correct false impressions that even textbooks themselves give of the Negro and his achievements. Through creative fellowship with his students he will help them toward a discovery and development of their latent powers.[8]

Conclusions. From the foregoing discussion it may be concluded that

7. L. R. Reynolds, "The Curriculum of the Liberal Arts College for Negroes and the Demands of a Bi-racial Society," *Quarterly Review of Higher Education among Negroes,* II (April, 1934), 102–108.

8. W. E. B. Du Bois, "Education and Work," *Journal of Negro Education,* I (January, 1932), 60–74.

the colleges of this study are, for the most part, concerned enough about providing special work in religion to employ a teacher or staff member who will have as one of his primary interests the responsibility of planning for the religious life of the campus.

The statistics cannot show, however, to what extent these workers in religion are given enough freedom from heavy teaching and other responsibilities to allow them time for the working out of a program that would in a real way be effective for the students as a whole. The writer knows from personal experiences and contacts that the director of religious activities in many of the colleges is quite overburdened with work and does not have either time or the energy to put himself unstintedly into the task. In some instances, besides having a full teaching program, directing religious activities, and supervising religious organizations, he must serve on other committees and help to direct other extracurricular activities of the college as well.

It is not contended here that the director of religious life should have no teaching responsibilities at all. Three of the 33 workers in this study have no teaching load and two have only minor teaching responsibility. Some teaching by the religious director is desirable for the purpose of establishing academic status and prestige. But, when the work of directing religious activities is tacked on to the responsibilities of an already overburdened teacher, it seems to imply that religion is not important enough to rate a full-time staff member who will work out and carry forward an adequate program as well as symbolize the importance which the college attaches to the place of religion in its total scheme. In spite of this difficulty the data of the directors of religious life reveal that from the point of view of chronological maturity, scholastic preparation, and academic rank these men are relatively well trained for the responsibility that is theirs.

VI

COURSE OFFERINGS IN RELIGION

T HE course offerings in religion in Negro higher institutions should be seen in the light of the broader problems incidental to the curriculum of the Negro college. Harap defines the curriculum as follows: "The word *curriculum* is Latin for race-course, or the race itself— a place of deeds, or a series of deeds. *As applied to education it is that series of things which children and youth must do and experience* by way of developing ability to do the things well that make up the affairs of adult life." [1] This view of the curriculum is perhaps the dominant one in American education at the present time, except for the fact that there are many who would not emphasize the last phrase, "ability to do the things well that make up the affairs of adult life," for this attitude tends to neglect the value of childhood personality for its own sake. The curriculum is best understood when the place of the experience of the individual in the learning process is taken more fully into account. Thus the curriculum is variously spoken of as the "experiences of the learner under guidance," or as "enriched and controlled experience." [2] This means that the school, once having determined its educational objectives, has as its next most important problem the provision of the various experiences "under guidance" through which the individual must pass in order to reach the desirable goals. The curriculum in this sense grows out of the purpose of the school.

The Negro "functional college" and the curriculum. Such a concept of the curriculum as given above is obviously functional and dynamic and lends itself well to the philosophy of education which views the educational process as rooted in the current social milieu. One Negro college thus makes the statement in its catalogue that

The College does not bifurcate its curriculum offerings into "regular" and "extra" curriculum activities. Emphasis is upon providing an integrated and vital educational environment to the end that each member of its community may be stimulated into that type of growth which will reflect an increasing achievement of moral and spiritual values. Every course involves some form of expressional activity through classroom instruction. There are only "curriculum" activities. The activities fostered rep-

1. Quoted by H. L. Caswell and D. S. Campbell, *Curriculum Development* (New York, American Book Co., 1935), pp. 66–67.
2. W. C. Bower, *The Curriculum of Religious Education* (New York, Charles Scribner's Sons, 1925), chap. iv.

resent an integral part of the several courses within the four general Divisions of Instruction.[3]

In the spirit of this principle, Gallagher after analyzing and rejecting several suggested plans of determining the curricula of colleges proposes a functional curriculum, based on the idea that "education gets its meaning and sense of direction from its purposive effort to build better life for all; and this places first emphasis upon attitude. Only in the light of such an inclusive societal framework can we have an adequate notion of the needs of the individual. . . . Intended social functioning becomes the larger framework for educational construction." [4]

Along somewhat the same thought, Loram, in his Hampton commencement address on "New Opportunities for the Negro College," suggests that Negro colleges proceed along the lines of real progressive education, where methods employed in the educational process are selected on the basis of their being able to help the pupil more adequately to achieve the desired ends. In elaborating on the meaning of this idea, Loram says, "The essence of real progressive education is discipline—the only real discipline, the discipline that comes from within, the discipline that springs from a *respect for human personality both in ourselves and in others* . . . It is towards the self-disciplined freedom involved in progressive education that the Negro college must remove." [5] Continuing, Loram urges that the private Negro college should take advantage of the relative freedom it enjoys and carry forward needed work in experimental projects. From such activity it is assumed that better curricula and desirable experiences might be provided for the Negro college student. Since relatively few Negro institutions are doing significant work along the line of experimental education, the suggestion above is particularly well taken.

General course offerings in Negro colleges. A study of the development of course offerings in colleges for Negroes shows that, in general, they have followed the trend set by the white colleges of the nation. Earlier in this study attention was called to the way in which the founders of the colleges, soon after the Civil War, attempted to establish for the freedmen the same kind of educational facilities that the founders themselves had known and experienced in the colleges of the North and East. After the basic foundations had gradually been laid in the elementary and secondary education of Negroes, the colleges were not long in adopting practically without change the course offerings that were given in other col-

3. Philander Smith College, *Catalogue*, May, 1939, p. 22.
4. B. G. Gallagher, *American Caste and the Negro College* (New York, Columbia University Press, 1938), p. 344.
5. Charles T. Loram, "New Opportunities for the Negro College," *Southern Workman*, LXIII (June, 1934), p. 174. (Italics mine.)

leges of the nation. For example, as late as 1931 Knox found that "the academic courses in the liberal arts colleges of this study are patterned after the leading American colleges, and reliable and competent textbooks are used." [6]

Whatever changes have occurred in this part of the college curriculum have usually followed the general trend of changes occurring elsewhere. Armstrong [7] found that before 1900 the content of the Negro college curriculum was "predominantly classic with some science and mathematics." Within the next ten years, however, courses in the social sciences and in modern languages had practically taken precedence over the traditional classical subjects. For concrete analysis he made a study of the courses given in a typical Negro liberal arts college and found that from 1925 to 1935 "fifteen times the number of courses in modern languages were given as compared to the number during the first decade of the college's existence." Considerably fewer courses in the classics were offered at this later time. Between 1933 and 1935 there were 16 courses in philosophy and psychology offered. A total of 400 courses, however, was offered in the social sciences, representing the largest percentage of increase in course offerings between 1927 and 1935. Courses in English and in the natural sciences increased greatly. Because of the many students going into teaching, a large number of courses were offered in this field. In the eight-year period ending in 1935 some 214 courses were given in education. Of late there have been other courses such as journalism and business administration added to the courses of study. These facts indicate something of the general trend in the course offerings of Negro colleges. A broader study by Armstrong showed the following results:

In 1936 the composite picture of the program offerings of six colleges placed English first with 22 courses, education with seventeen, history and mathematics with 12 each, biology, chemistry and French with eleven each, music and economics with ten each. Greek, Latin and agriculture came at the end of the list. The offerings included such subjects as home economics, physical education, politics and art, which indicate the variety of interests, and suggest an adaptation to present general tendencies toward a broad curriculum. [8]

These statistics demonstrate that, for the most part, if the colleges for Negroes have felt that they have a particular set of objectives to accomplish that differs at all from the objectives of the other colleges of the

6. Ellis O. Knox, "The Trend of Progress in the Light of New Educational Concepts in a Group of American Colleges Dominated by Religious Influences" (Ph.D. dissertation, University of Southern California, Los Angeles, 1931).

7. B. K. Armstrong, "Factors in the Formulation of a Collegiate Program for Negroes" (Ph.D. dissertation, University of Michigan, Ann Arbor, 1938).

8. *Ibid.*, chap. vi.

nation, they have not provided any unusual type of course offerings to help reach these ends which may be peculiar to the Negro college. Of course it is quite possible that the name or title of a course may offer no real indication of the particular slant which the instructor gives to the subject. It is no doubt true that American history taught in a Negro school, for example, by a Negro professor will have an emphasis in many cases that helps the Negro student toward the kind of social adjustment he needs which he may not receive if he takes the same course, as far as title, period covered, and even textbook are concerned, under other circumstances.

The significance of courses in religion. It is a basic assumption of this study that religion should have a fundamental place in education because of the age-long conviction of the human spirit that religion is vital to man's life. Religion is not only "caught," it is "taught." It is not a matter merely of emotional reactions but also a question of the application of the intellectual processes essential to the acquisition of truth in general. The fund of information concerning religion which has been gathered through the centuries can be used in much the same way as the accumulated experiences in the social and natural sciences can be used. Writing on this subject, Bond states, "There is sufficient universality and objectivity in religious experience, both individual and social, to enable scholars to organize and classify a large body of data from which certain generalizations may be drawn and on the basis of which broad, fundamental concepts can be built." [9]

The vast amount of information in such fields as Biblical literature and the history of religion can be useful in broadening the mind of the student and helping him to understand the nature and background of the culture in which he lives. Other subjects such as the psychology of religion and the philosophy of religion may be useful in helping the student to see the relation of religion to the various areas of man's life and thought.

Moreover, if it is recognized also that religion is a way of life and may well be defined in "terms of a life devoted to the highest values," [10] then the attempt to teach religion effectively immediately takes on new responsibilities. The teaching of values and appreciations in religion ought to be the responsibility of the college as well as of the church. Recognizing the historical association of religion with the good life, the college may guide students into an appreciation of the great contributions to history that have grown out of man's devotion to the good.

9. C. H. Bond, *The Liberal Arts College Functioning in the Field of Religion,* The National Council on Religion in Higher Education, Bulletin X (New York, 1935), p. 21.
10. J. S. Bixler, *Can Religion Be Taught?* The National Council on Religion in Higher Education, Bulletin IX (New York, 1935), p. 16.

Not the least important, therefore, of the ways in which the college may recognize its responsibility to society in mediating to the student the fruits and values in religion as a cultural phenomenon is for the college to include courses in religious subjects in its curriculum. The courses in religion will form the intellectual basis upon which the student may build his religious world view.

The kind of religious background in which the average Negro college student lives is one that is characterized by traditional, otherworldly religious concepts. It is partly because of this that one agrees with the statement made by Mays, quoted earlier, in discussing the religious needs of Negro college students. He asserted that these students need to have "an intelligent understanding of the Bible and a fair knowledge of the historical development of the Christian religion." Obviously this need is common to all students regardless of race, but the background of Negro life and religion make this need particularly relevant. Moreover, it will largely be through courses in religion that many of the psychogenic handicaps of caste status will be overcome.

In the light of this assumption, it was undertaken in the present study to discover the extent of religious instruction in the colleges for Negroes. Data were secured from 45 colleges, of which 19 were church related, 4 private, and 22 supported by public funds. The data are largely for the school years 1939–40 and 1940–41.

Credit courses in religion. Credit courses in religion were offered in 25, or 55 per cent, of the 45 institutions reporting. A total of 20 institutions offered no credit courses in religion. Nineteen of these latter were public institutions and one was private. While this private institution offered no courses for college credit, it did offer systematic studies in religion at the weekly Sunday-school hour which were compulsory for freshmen and sophomores. Likewise, one public institution sponsored a regular Sunday school compulsory for the underclassmen in which a large number of courses in religion were provided, including a course in teacher training.

If it is true that courses in religion are fundamental for the development of the most desirable life attitudes as well as for bridging some of the barriers of caste, it is of more than passing significance that in 45 per cent of the colleges of this study no such courses were offered for college credit. Most of these were public institutions and one must conclude that because more than 50 per cent of the collegiate population among Negroes is in those schools there is a serious lack of opportunity for adequate spiritual preparation for life through the taking of courses in religious study.

Number of courses and semester hours offered. The 25 colleges having courses in religion for college credit offered an aggregate of 207 courses ranging from 1 to 18 per college. The aggregate number of semester hours which the institutions offered in religion was 620, or an average of 24.8 hours per college. The 19 church-related schools offered a total of 178 courses totaling 535 semester hours, averaging 28.8 hours for each institution.

Of the 25 institutions providing religious courses, 14, or 56 per cent, provided a major in the field. Twelve of the institutions were church related and 2 were under private control.

Types of courses offered. On the whole, the list of courses in religion offered in the colleges of this study indicates a fairly wide variety of selections. An examination of the courses offered reveals that those in Bible as well as religious education take precedence over all others. Table VII shows the various fields in which courses are offered and the frequency with which each one is listed in the three types of colleges.

TABLE VII

NUMBER OF COURSES IN RELIGIOUS SUBJECTS ACCORDING TO TYPE OF COLLEGE AND NAME OF SUBJECT

Subjects	Total Number of Courses	Per-centage	Type of Institution Church	Private	Public	Number Required
Number of Institutions			19	3	3	
Bible	65	31.2	54	9	2	16
Religious Education	45	21.8	41	3	1	3
History, Philosophy, and Psychology of Religion	30	14.5	27	1	2	–
Church History	19	9.3	18	1	–	–
Christian Ethics	8	3.9	6	2	–	–
Religious Problems	7	3.4	5	1	1	–
The Church and Society	6	3.0	4	2	–	–
The Negro Church	2	.9	1	–	1	–
Missions	2	.9	2	–	–	–
Ethics and Philosophy	16	7.7	14	–	2	4
Unclassified	7	3.4	6	–	1	6
Total	207	100.0	178	19	10	29

Courses in Bible rank first among the types of courses offered, with a total of 65 courses listed in this field. This is 31.2 per cent of the total number of courses reported and is also approximately 20 per cent higher than courses in religious education which rank second. It is of interest to observe the areas upon which emphasis is put in Bible study. A total of 14 courses were in the field of the life and teachings of Jesus, 9 had to do with some phase of New Testament interpretation, and 16 were concerned with Old Testament studies. The remaining 21 courses were general Biblical studies.

Forty-five, or 21.8 per cent, of the total number of courses were in the field of religious education. This suggests that, at least for the schools of this study, one of the primary objectives in offering courses in religion was preparation of church-school workers. The third ranking group of courses was those in the history, psychology, and philosophy of religion. Thirty, or 14.5 per cent, of the total number of courses were classified in this group. It is significant that this field of study should rank relatively high. Through courses dealing with these subjects it is possible for meaningful interpretations of the significance of religion for personal adjustment to be given. Although courses in church history rank fourth on the list, 7 of the 19 courses listed in this field were given in one college.

It is also noteworthy that some of the colleges are including courses having to do with the practical application of religion to present social and personal problems. Eight courses were in the field of Christian ethics. Six others dealt with the church and society. Typical among the titles of such courses were "Christianity and Society" and the "Church and Social Problems." Seven courses were found that could be classified under the general heading of religious problems. Here it is clear that some colleges are attempting to meet the needs which often appear when the student is perplexed by the problems incident to the breakdown of the religious concepts which he brings to college.

Two institutions reported courses dealing with the Negro church. It is probably true that an attempt is being made here to demonstrate the significance of this important social institution for the total life of the Negro caste. If this is true, opportunity for bridging some of the barriers of caste through practical programs of the Negro church should be made increasingly manifest, for certainly it will be largely through organized religion that many of the racial problems will be solved.

Sixteen courses in ethics and philosophy were offered by the 25 schools of this study. All except 2 of these were given in church-related institutions. Ten of the courses were in logic, history of and introduction to philosophy, while 6 dealt with general ethics.

Wickey and Eckhart found in their study of the offerings in religion in all the colleges of the country that "The 334 Protestant colleges give 2,425 religious courses, of which 971, or 40%, are Bible courses; 267, or 11%, are religious education, and 348, or 14%, deal with the history, psychology, and philosophy of religion." [11] It is apparent that although the Negro institutions of this study do not offer as large a percentage of courses in Bible as was true of the colleges and institutions of the country at large in 1935, the greatest emphasis in each case was upon Biblical studies.

11. G. Wickey and R. A. Eckhart, "A National Survey of Courses in Bible and Religion," *Christian Education*, XX (October, 1936), 28.

Whereas, in the Wickey and Eckhart study the courses in Bible constituted 40 per cent of the total number of religious courses offered, courses
in this area constituted 31.2 per cent of the religious courses in the schools
of this study. But 11 per cent of the courses in the national survey were
in religious education, while 21.8 per cent of the 207 courses in the present survey were in this field. Again, while the courses in the history, psychology, and philosophy of religion ranked second in the national survey
with 14 per cent of the total in this field, these courses ranked third in
the present survey, but the proportion was about the same.

Religious course requirements for graduation. There was a time when
the large majority of Negro schools required religious courses for graduation. Reference to Table VII, on page 81, shows that if the figures from the
colleges of this study are typical, this majority is now somewhat reduced.
Sixteen, or 64 per cent, of the 25 colleges offering religious courses required courses in religion for graduation. These 16 schools required a
total of 29 courses in religion which were given for an aggregate of 87
semester hours or for an average of between 3 and 4 semester hours per
college. The range of hours required was from 2 to 8. Four of the church-
related colleges and 2 of the private institutions made no requirements
for taking religious courses. None of the 3 public colleges made any requirements in this field. The 29 required courses constituted only 14 per
cent of the total number of courses offered. Stated another way, 86 per cent
of the religious courses offered for credit in the 25 colleges were elective.

According to the Wickey and Eckhart study, 82.2 per cent of the Protestant colleges of the country made requirements of courses in Bible and
religion for graduation.[12] The figures for the present survey show that
64 per cent of the church and private colleges made such requirements.
It is probable that if statistics were available for all the church and private colleges for Negroes, the percentage of those making requirements
for taking religious courses for graduation would be somewhat higher.

The 29 required courses for which names were given were in 12 different subjects, chief among which were general studies in the Bible.
Nine, or 31 per cent, of the total number of required courses were in this
field. Three courses were listed as required in each of the following fields:
history of religion (including comparative religion), the life and teachings of Jesus, ethics, and religious education. Although religious education was second in the total number of courses offered, only 3 courses in
this field were required.

Statistics on the enrollment in religious courses. It was difficult to secure comprehensive figures on the enrollment in the courses in religion,
since several of the respondents failed to answer this section of the ques-

12. *Ibid.*, p. 29.

tionnaire completely. The investigator hazards the opinion, however, that if the total figures were available the percentage results would not be essentially different from the ones at hand.

Seventeen colleges reported a grand total enrollment in 120 religious courses of 3,782 students, an average of 222.4 students per college. This figure as well as the others having to do with enrollment undoubtedly includes some duplications of the same students taking more than one religious course in the same semester or in the same year. The average number of students enrolled per course is 31.4. Twelve institutions showed a total enrollment in required courses of 1,819 students, averaging 91 students per course, and 17 colleges reported a total of 1,963 students enrolled in 100 elective courses.

Percentage of total enrollment of students taking work in religion. It is not possible in the present investigation to indicate the percentage of the total enrollment comprised by students taking courses in religion. It is significant, however, to consider the statistics of this study in connection with those of a survey made in 1935. From reports made to the Southern Association of Colleges and Secondary Schools by its member institutions, McCuiston [13] listed the total number of courses offered, the total enrollment in all courses, and the percentage registered in each type of course. The first 9 courses enrolling the largest percentage of students were, in order, English and speech, education and psychology, physical education, history and government, biology, chemistry, French, mathematics, and sociology. Religion and philosophy ranked tenth in the number of students enrolled. Sixty-nine courses in religion and philosophy were offered by the schools reporting. The total enrollment in these courses was 1,666 students, representing 3 per cent of the total enrollment in all courses.

Since the percentages of McCuiston's study are computed on the basis of all the colleges making reports, which includes a large number of public colleges in which no credit courses in religion are offered, it is evident that if the computation were made on the basis of only those colleges actually offering courses in religion and philosophy, the percentage of the total enrollment of students in all courses who are taking courses in religion would be much higher. The findings of the present study show an average enrollment per course of 31.5 students. In the study by McCuiston, the average enrollment per course for the 69 courses listed in religion and philosophy was 24.7. It is apparent that the findings of the present study regarding enrollment in religious courses are fairly closely related to those in McCuiston's investigation.

Yet, in view of the importance which is assumed here of the academic

13. Fred S. McCuiston, *Graduate Instruction for Negroes in the United States* (Nashville, George Peabody College for Teachers, 1939), Table VIII.

study of religion, as well as in the light of the interest which students themselves have in religious values, the fact that only 3 per cent of the total enrollment was in courses in religion and philosophy is of great importance. It means, among other things, that a great many Negro students are deprived of the opportunity to receive college training in one of the most important, if not the most important, of the subjects conducive to the formation and development of significant life attitudes. Obviously, such attitudes are necessary for all members of the population, those who are leaders in the professional life as well as the skilled tradesmen, artisans, and laborers.

Enrollment in religious courses according to subject of study. In Table VIII are given the enrollment averages for each course for which a total registration of more than 10 was reported. In view of the fact that the majority of the courses were Biblical, it is expected that the largest enrollment would be in this area. Fifty-eight per cent of the enrollment in the 120 courses for which enrollments were reported was in some aspect of Bible study. Part of the explanation of this large figure is that the majority of the required courses were in this field. The second largest total enrollment was in religious education; 550 students were reported enrolled in 30 courses in this area. This represents 14.5 per cent of the total enrollment in all religious courses. Thirteen courses in ethics and philosophy enrolled 301 students representing 8 per cent of the total enrollment in religious courses. The fourth ranking courses were those in the history,

TABLE VIII

ENROLLMENT IN RELIGIOUS COURSES ARRANGED BY SUBJECTS

Subjects	Number of Courses Reported	Total Enrollment	Percentage of Total	Average per Course
Bible	39	2,195	58.0	51
Religious Education	30	550	14.5	18
History, Philosophy and Psychology of Religion	17	271	7.2	23
Church History	8	163	4.3	20
Christian Ethics	3	72	1.9	24
Religious Problems	2	26	.7	13
The Church and Society	3	55	1.4	18
The Negro Church	1	30	.8	3
Missions	1	10	.3	10
Ethics and Philosophy	13	301	8.0	26
Unclassified	3	109	2.9	36
Total	120	3,782	100.00	31.5

philosophy, and psychology of religion, in which were included 7.2 per cent of the total enrollment.

Of the courses in which no requirements for attendance are listed, those in the history, philosophy, and psychology of religion ranked first in percentage of total enrollment. In 17 courses in these fields there was an average enrollment of 23 students per course. Second in this group was church history in which there was an average attendance of 20 students listed in the 8 courses. It appears that when students are allowed to elect courses they are likely to elect those dealing with the interpretation and the history of religion. This is the point at which many students feel a need.

Religious courses in state institutions. The absence of courses in religion in a large number of tax-supported institutions may mean that, as in a number of known cases, the administrators feel that there are legal restrictions against the teaching of religion in their schools. In Searles's study, however, it was found that in only 7 states were there constitutional prohibitions against the teaching of religion in public schools and in only 4 states were there legislative provisions against it.[14] In only 2 of the states having constitutional provisions against the teaching of religion were Negro colleges located, and in only 1 state having legislative provision were there Negro institutions. If this is true, there is little legal reason why more Negro colleges should not proceed to teach courses in religion in connection with their regular college curriculum. The extra efforts and costs involved in providing the additional staff members for the teaching of religion may act as a deterrent to some administrators of public colleges. Since the public colleges for Negroes are enrolling increasingly larger numbers of Negro students so that at the present time they account for at least half of the total collegiate population of this group, it becomes even more desirable to explore the possibilities for including an adequate program of religious instruction in these institutions. It is not enough to rely, as some administrators do, on the mediation of religion to students through occasional chapel talks on religion. As M. L. Jacks maintains, if there is to be any practical application of the principles of religion in the life of the individual and of society, those principles of religion must be inculcated during the regular educational process.[15]

14. Herbert L. Searles, *State Constitutional and Legislative Provisions and Supreme Court Decisions Relating to Sectarian Religious Influence in Tax-Supported Universities, Colleges and Public Schools,* The National Council on Religion in Higher Education, Bulletin V (New York, 1924), pp. 5, 13.

15. M. L. Jacks, *God in Education* (London, Rich & Cowan, 1939), p. xii.

VII

VOLUNTARY STUDENT RELIGIOUS ORGANIZATIONS

THE banding of themselves in voluntary religious organizations has been characteristic of students in American education for more than two hundred years. In fact, as Shedd points out, there is hardly anything that has characterized student life more than this tendency to originate and maintain groups for the development of the religious life.[1] This fact has served as evidence of the spiritual longing that is common to the race, a longing that is never quite overshadowed by academic pursuits or extracurricular activities of college life.

A study of the voluntary religious organizations and programs of students in the colleges for Negro youth reveals that among them is likewise expressed the desire for the realization of the larger life to be found in religious fellowship.

Development of student religious organizations. When the movement for the establishment of Negro colleges was born the Student Christian Movement in the colleges was already rapidly on the way to becoming of age. It was natural, therefore, that relatively early in the life of the Negro college the student religious organizations should take the name as well as the organizational pattern of the Christian Associations predominant in American colleges. In 1869, only two years after Howard University, Washington, D.C., opened its doors, a Young Men's Christian Association was organized among the students. The work of the eleven students who participated in this organization represents the first Young Men's Christian Association to be established on the campus of a Negro college. The object of the organization was "to exert a Christian influence among our unconverted fellow students, and to promote our own growth in holiness. The greater portion of us occupy our time on the Lord's Day in teaching Sabbath-school classes, and in other Christian work." [2]

Three Negro colleges, Howard, Fisk, and Walden, had representatives at the historic meeting in Louisville, Kentucky, when the Intercollegiate Young Men's Christian Association was born in 1877. Several other colleges were represented two years later when the International Young Men's Christian Association Movement Convention was held in Baltimore, Maryland. It is significant that by this time the movement among Negro

1. C. P. Shedd, *Two Centuries of Student Christian Movements* (New York, Association Press, 1934), p. xvii.
2. *Association Monthly*, January, 1870, p. 140 (quoted by Shedd, *op. cit.*, p. 109).

students had developed so rapidly that this convention appointed Henry E. Brown as the first secretary for work among Negro students.[3] The number of associations grew from 18 in 1886 to 61 by 1900. In the latter year student conferences were held in three Negro colleges. Twelve years later there were reported 103 associations in Negro colleges and at this time, June, 1912, the first summer Young Men's Christian Association conference of Negro students was held at King's Mountain, North Carolina. Later joined by the Young Women's Christian Association, this conference continued as the main Negro student Christian conference until the delegates voted at the meeting in 1937 to discontinue having an exclusively Negro conference and to make it open to any student in the region who wished to attend. Since that time the conference has met on an interracial basis at Talladega College, Alabama.

The rise of the Christian Associations in the colleges for Negroes has paralleled the rise of the colleges themselves. The spread of the movement was rapid and in time the Student Christian Associations became the most influential organizations in the lives of the students. The outstanding students took the leadership in these groups, just as the outstanding adults took places of leadership in the life of the church.

The present status of voluntary religious groups. The present status of student religious organizations in the colleges for Negroes is characterized by similarities in other schools. In addition to the Young Men's and Young Women's Christian Associations, there are to be found coeducational Christian Associations as well as miscellaneous religious organizations of a local nature.[4] In all but one of the 44 schools giving data on student organizations are to be found one or more voluntary student religious groups. This lone institution was a municipal college, 25 per cent of the enrollment of which was Catholic. There is an average of 3 student religious organizations per college for the institutions reporting such groups. The predominant organizations are the Young Men's and the Young Women's Christian Associations. Nine institutions reported coeducational Christian Associations.

Types of organizations. In addition to the regular Christian Associations, the types of voluntary student religious organizations on the campuses of the colleges for Negroes include, among others, Sunday-school groups, ministerial clubs, fellowship groups, sectarian groups, and missionary societies. In Table IX is to be seen the distribution of these organizations arranged by type of college. Five of the schools with coeducational Student Christian Associations also reported having both a Y.M.C.A. and a Y.W.C.A. It is possible that in these schools, as in sev-

3. Shedd, *op. cit.*, p. 318 *et passim.*
4. The statistics for the present chapter come from 44 institutions, of which 19 were church-related, 4 private, and 21 public.

eral known cases, the two organizations maintain their organizational identity while the major part of their activities is on a joint basis.

As seen in Table IX, the organizations of ministerial students were found largely in church-related colleges. No such group was found in a state institution. On the other hand, the denominational groups were to be found wholly in state colleges. In one state college the administration has attempted to have students of the same denomination meet under the supervision of a local minister of each religious group. While the administration was apparently enthusiastic over the plan, the investigator gained the impression from talking with some of the undergraduate leaders that the students did not share this enthusiasm. The Newman clubs were found in those state colleges enrolling a considerable number of Catholics.

TABLE IX

STUDENT RELIGIOUS ORGANIZATIONS IN 44 COLLEGES ARRANGED BY TYPE OF COLLEGE

Name of Organization	Total	Church	Type of College Private	Public
1. Y.M.C.A.	36	16	2	18
2. Y.W.C.A.	36	17	1	18
3. Student Christian Association	9	2	2	5
4. Sunday-school Groups	9	5	–	4
5. Ministerial Groups	8	7	1	–
6. Religious Fellowship Groups	5	1	2	2
7. Protestant Groups	4	–	–	4 *
8. Newman Clubs	3	–	–	3
9. Missionary societies	2	1	–	1
10. Others	8	4	–	4
Total	120	53	8	59

* All in one college.

Membership in voluntary religious organizations. Although not all of the 42 schools supplied data with respect to the number of members in student religious organizations, information is available from a sufficient number to indicate the general trend. Nineteen colleges reported a total Y.M.C.A. membership of 2,445 students, an average of 128 students per school. At 8 of these institutions the students automatically have nominal membership by virtue of the fact that the budgetary provisions for the organization are taken from student activities fees. This type of automatic membership in Student Christian Associations has characterized the practice in colleges of both racial groups in the South. At least one reason why it is prevalent in Negro colleges is that the financial status of students makes it difficult to assure an adequate budget for voluntary organizations otherwise.

There are some difficulties associated in practice with this type of membership. The most serious drawback is that, not having to struggle to secure a budget, students are deprived of many of the spiritual values and practical experiences which accompany such efforts. Again, in such situations it is often difficult to elicit real interest and support for the program of the organization on the part of students. The organization is often taken for granted. Yet with competent faculty and student leadership many of the difficulties may be overcome.

In view of the automatic membership in the institutions reporting it in this study, a more accurate picture of the real student interest in voluntary religious organizations will be seen if the total and the average membership figures of those groups not having automatic membership are reported. Thus, in 12 colleges the total membership listed is 927 students, an average of 77 students per college. The number of members per organization ranged from 15 to 125.

Twenty-one colleges reported a total Y.M.C.A. membership of 2,071 students, an average of approximately 97 students for each organization. Omitting, however, the 2 institutions where membership is automatic, the total enrollment in 19 schools is 1,184, or an average of 62 students per organization. It is noted that there is less tendency to have automatic membership in the Y.W.C.A. than in the Y.M.C.A.

Sixteen miscellaneous organizations in 9 colleges reported memberships totaling 748 students, an average of 40 students per organization.

The total membership figures for all organizations is 5,928. This number, of course, contains duplicates of those students who are members of the Y.M.C.A. or of the Y.W.C.A. and are also members of additional religious organizations on the campus.

The membership figures given in the questionnaire are probably to be taken as estimates in some instances. It is quite likely that in many of these colleges the students who participate actively in the work of the Student Christian Associations and the other voluntary religious organizations are much smaller in number than the membership figures given.

Faculty advisers. The role of the faculty adviser to student organizations is one that carries with it many possibilities for personal guidance. With competent leadership of this type, the Negro student religious organizations should be directed to goals which will help toward the breakdown of some of the handicaps of a caste society. Practically all of the various student groups of this study have faculty sponsors. In several instances these are the personnel deans or the director of religious life. In many cases, however, the faculty advisers are members of the staff not connected with either the administrative or the official religious life of the campus. In most instances these adult leaders are appointed by the college president; occasionally they are selected by the students themselves.

One of the handicaps under which many of these faculty members work is that of being so engaged in other responsibilities that there is insufficient opportunity for them to work adequately with students. Only two of the institutions reported full-time staff members who were paid to work primarily with the student religious organizations. In these two schools there were coeducational student Christian organizations and there was more financial security than the majority of Negro colleges have. In other schools the faculty advisers were generally staff members whose major responsibilities were teaching or administrative work.

Types of activities. The various student religious organizations carry on a variety of activities. For the most part these activities are of a religious, educational, and social nature. The activity mentioned most frequently is forums. Thirty-two Student Christian Associations listed this as one of the regular features of their programs. This seems to indicate that in the colleges studied students are interested in the opportunity informally to discuss some of the current issues in discussion groups or debates.

By far the larger proportion of the activities of the Student Christian Associations has to do with some form of religious exercise. Twenty-eight of the organizations listed worship programs as one of their activities. Many of these were vesper programs given either on Sundays or during the week, while a few were listed simply as prayer meetings. In addition to these must be added the programs given during the chapel hour on week days which are generally of a religious nature. Seventeen organizations were said to present programs in the chapel as a part of their regular programs, although in some instances these opportunities occurred not more than once or twice a year. Only five of the Student Christian Associations sponsor Sunday-school or Bible study groups and three of these were in state colleges. In one state institution, a college with over 900 students enrolled, students organized a Bible class which meets each Sunday night following the regular compulsory chapel service. Attendance is said to range from 60 to 80 students regularly. Although the name of the organization is "Bible Class," most of the subjects listed for discussion at the time of the investigation had to do with the nature and characteristics of various religions of the world. The enthusiasm with which the students have supported this organization is indicative of the interest college youth have in religion under the stimulus of adequate student leadership.

That the students in these colleges have some interest in social service is indicated by the fact that twenty-six organizations of the Christian Association mentioned this as one of their regular features. Included in the term "social service" are such activities as giving baskets of food to the poor during the Thanksgiving and Christmas seasons, collecting old clothes for poverty-stricken families in slum areas, and conducting Sunday-school classes in such communities. The Student Christian Associations are interested also in recreational and social activities. Nineteen organizations were listed as providing some kind of recreational program, including athletic enterprises.

Besides these activities, the Student Christian Associations sponsor programs for freshman orientation, holiday celebrations, annual retreats, exchange programs with other college associations, and coöperation with churches in the local community.

A review of the activities of the miscellaneous student organizations reveals a similarity between them and those of the Student Christian Associations. Here religious programs take precedence over other types of activities. Only a few additional types of activities are mentioned. These have to do mainly with discussion groups and charity work in the local community. These additional organizations supplement on each campus the work of the Student Christian Associations. The organized groups of students who are looking forward to the ministry carry on programs which give them some sense of professional fellowship as well as practical experience in the delivery of sermons and in theological discussion.

Student conferences. One of the important activities reported by student organizations is participation in intercollegiate conferences. Some of the conferences reported were local; others were area or regional summer gatherings. The conferences to which the largest number of students went were the King's Mountain and Talladega meetings which have represented the Student Christian Movement assembly for Southern Negro students. In an earlier discussion it has been pointed out that the Negro students at the 1937 King's Mountain conference voted to discontinue meeting on a strictly interracial basis. The subsequent summer conferences to which Negro students go have been held at Talladega College, Alabama, and have been strictly interracial meetings, although the proportion of white students attending them has not been as large as that of Negro students. One other interracial Student Movement conference which four institutions reported was the Hollister, Missouri, conference. It is of importance to note that this conference meeting in the Southwest area has been able to operate on an interracial basis for several years and represents a distinct advance in breaking down some of the interracial barriers characteristic of the South. There are those who have sought continuously to have all Christian Association students in the Southeast meet on a similar interracial basis. The Talladega conference has been the nearest approach to this ideal. Although the difficulties incidental to the total realization of joint meetings are rather severe it is not beyond the realm of possibility that this will materialize eventually if the present progress in that direction continues.

Most of the other student conferences listed are of an interracial nature and, to the extent that these meetings are carefully planned, they afford opportunities of immeasurable value for the much-needed development of mutual understanding between Negro and white students. Many are the testimonies from students who have had their first awakening to the significance of interracial understanding and appreciation stimulated by attendance at such a gathering. When students as well as adults of both races are able to come together and discuss objectively the problems common to both groups, it is then that the way is opened for bridging some of the most difficult psychogenic and sociological barriers imposed by the caste system. Increasingly colleges should provide these opportunities for intercollegiate interracial conferences.

The "church following its students." One of the significant findings of this study is that the organized church groups have generally not seen fit to follow the Negro students in state institutions. A promising beginning has been made in recent years in at least two institutions, the Fort Valley State College, Georgia, and the Morgan State College, Maryland. In both of these instances the impetus for the establishment of this work began when the state took over the college which had been originally under church auspices. The establishment at Fort Valley State College, Georgia, of the Fort Valley College Center in 1940 represents the pioneer project of this kind in the education of Negroes. With a fine physical plant adequately staffed, this center operates under the control of the Episcopal Church which transferred the college property to the state of Georgia. Activities of various kinds are promoted, with special emphasis upon meeting the needs of the Episcopal students not only in the college but in the geographical region in which the college is located. Although this center in principle ministers to the needs of all the students in the college which it adjoins, there is a strong possibility that its influence is seriously limited because of the denominational interest which underlies the total program.

The Morgan College Center, Baltimore, Maryland, was established in 1941 at Morgan State College by the Methodist Church. This represents the effort on the part of that denominational group to maintain the religious tradition that had been associated with the college until it was transferred to the state of Maryland. Here, too, a fine building has been erected and a trained, full-time director is employed. The organizational setup is that of the Wesley Foundations.

Both of these projects represent significant beginnings in the possibilities of organized religious work in state colleges for Negroes. Because the enrollment in these colleges is relatively small, the effectiveness of this type of project would be greatly enhanced if the controlling denominations would invite the active coöperation of other denominational educational boards in carrying forward the work. The time is ripe for the Negro church as a whole to realize the importance of supplementing the religious program which the state colleges are able to provide.

Conclusions. Merely from the statistics given in this chapter it is difficult adequately to estimate the significance of the work of the voluntary religious organizations among Negro students. From personal observations, confirmed by statements of competent resident and traveling observers, the Christian Associations on some campuses are the most effective student organizations of all. These, however, may not be in the majority. It was not possible for the investigator to remain on the campuses of the colleges he visited long enough adequately to estimate the real influence which these organizations exert in the lives of the students as a whole. One is inclined to the view that this influence is often greater than the bare statistics lead one to believe. In the questionnaire study of the attitudes of students toward the religious life of the campus, several of the students said that the Student Christian Association was one of the helpful influences to them in the development of their religious and ethical life.

At the present time the student religious organization has many more competing factors in the campus situation than was true a generation ago. In order to insure the necessary resources for carrying on the life of the Christian Association some colleges have adopted the policy of including the Y.M.C.A. and the Y.W.C.A. in the organizations for which student activities fees are collected. This virtually means that students are compelled to support the religious organization whether they want to or not. Some students are found who resent this practice. Yet it is obvious in many cases that without such assurance of support the work of the religious organization would be most seriously handicapped. On the other hand, where students are led to join the Christian Association primarily because of the opportunity it offers them to develop their religious life and to contribute constructively to the life of the campus and to the larger Christian fellowship, the situation is a much more wholesome one for all concerned; for here the student, having voluntarily paid his membership fee, demonstrates his real interest in the work of the association and is much more likely to participate effectively in the program of the organization.

If the college administration will more adequately support the work of the Student Christian Association through the provision of faculty persons who are sufficiently relieved of other responsibilities effectively to give of their time and energies to the work of helping the students to develop a religious program which meets their needs, obviously the work of the religious groups on the campus will be greatly strengthened. Modern life offers the student so many opportunities and temptations to deviate from the ideals for which religion stands that unless the college makes every effort possible to counteract the secular influences and to develop along constructive lines the latent idealism common to all youth, it will pass up one of its most significant opportunities for the effective education of students. Moreover, the possibilities inherent in intercollegiate and interracial associations suggest that the student religious organizations may prove to be some of the major forces in higher education for the realization of the students' spiritual and social needs growing out of a biracial society.

VIII

BUDGETARY PROVISIONS FOR RELIGIOUS WORK BY COLLEGE ADMINISTRATIONS AND STUDENT RELIGIOUS ORGANIZATIONS

ARLIER in this study it was pointed out that if the statements given by college presidents and other officials in interviews are to be taken as representative, then it can be said that the presidents of the colleges for Negroes are committed to the assumption that religion has a most important role to play in the education of Negro youth. One of the standard indexes to the extent of interest the officials of any organization have in a project is the amount of money they are willing to invest in it. The question of how much money is actually expended for religious work on the campus becomes, therefore, one of the major items for consideration in a study of religion in higher education among Negroes.

It is not assumed here, however, that the expenditures for religious work on the campus are to be taken as a final measure of the real interest in religion on the part of college administrators. It is quite possible that, while interest in this area may be extensive, the authorities may not see the necessity nor the advisability for certain minimum appropriations for religion. It is also true, as was brought out in interviews with at least two presidents of state institutions, that the interest in religious work on the campus may be keen but the lack of adequate appropriations by state legislatures or other controlling agencies may prevent anything more than a minimum of emphasis to be given to this aspect of the college program.

Financial status of Negro colleges. Thus the religious budgets of the colleges must be seen in the light of their total financial status. No statistics regarding the gross income and expenditures of the individual colleges submitting data in this study are available. Figures are at hand, however, which give in general the financial status of Negro institutions as a whole. McCuiston's study [1] shows that the average income of the 58 private and denominational colleges reporting for that year was $68,080, while for the 33 public institutions it was $142,060. McCuiston's study also indicates that, while income from public sources has been gradually increasing, income from church sources shows a constant decline. In view of the fact that "only 5 Negro colleges have endowments of more than

1. Fred S. McCuiston, *Graduate Instruction for Negroes in the United States* (Nashville, George Peabody College for Teachers, 1939), pp. 23, 25 *et passim.*

$1,000,000, and that only 3 of these receive substantial income from this source," it is apparent that the general development of institutions of higher education for Negroes must of necessity be limited at many points.

Yet, the total effectiveness of the religious program cannot be accurately measured in terms of the amount of money actually spent for religious purposes. There are instances where a relatively small amount is available for religious work, but the careful planning as well as the fine personal qualifications of the college staff result in a much more effective religious program than sometimes follows when a larger amount of money is spent without careful planning and in a college community lacking the kind of *esprit de corps* necessary for a wholesome religious environment.

In this connection, a remark made by the president of a private college is particularly suggestive. This official said that it is assumed that the total budget of the college is thought of as a budget for religious work. Of course such a philosophy is sound in the final analysis, where the ultimate objectives of the college are conceived in essentially religious terms. It is nevertheless true that unless particular attention is given to certain provisions both curricular and extracurricular in scope, the effective presentation of religion to youth will be seriously curtailed.

Total budget for religious work.[2] The college officials were asked to indicate on the schedule the amount of money budgeted for the school year 1940–41. In some cases the amount listed represented an accurate statement of the money actually to be spent. In other cases only estimates could be had in regard to certain items. Again, some colleges listed gross expenditures for religious work, including the amount budgeted for such facilities as the upkeep of buildings or of rooms used for religious activities, traveling fees of faculty staff working in the field of religion, and secretarial help. On the basis of these facts it is reasonable to assume that, if all the institutions had listed the gross amount to be spent, the total budgets for the 31 colleges would be somewhat larger than they appear.

Table X, on page 98, exhibits a summary of the budget provisions for religious work by the college administrations in 31 institutions. These 31 institutions appropriated a total amount of $101,248.74 for religious work, an average of $3,266.03 per college. The figures show that the private colleges spent more than twice as much proportionally as the colleges

2. The data for the present study of college appropriations for religious work came from 31 institutions, of which 16 were church-related, 4 private, and 11 public. Twenty of the colleges were accredited Class A, and 11 others were either Class B or unaccredited. All of the private colleges were Class A, while of the 16 remaining institutions with this accreditation, 8 were church-related and 8 were under public control. These 31 colleges represent approximately 29 per cent of the total number of Negro colleges in America.

taken as a whole; while, as would be expected, the state colleges spent the least amount proportionally. The 4 private institutions appropriated a total of $30,515 for religious work during 1940–41, an average of more than $7,628 per college. At the same time, the 16 church-related colleges appropriated a total amount of $54,978.74 per college. This is less than half the average amount per college budgeted by the private colleges but is also nearly 3 times more than the average amount budgeted for religious work by the public institutions.

TABLE X

BUDGETARY PROVISIONS FOR RELIGIOUS WORK BY THE COLLEGE ADMINISTRATORS IN 31 COLLEGES

Type of College	Total Number of Colleges	Total Budget	Average Amount per College
Church-related			
Class A	8	$32,581.74	$4,071.46
Others	8	$22,397.00	$2,799.62
Total	16	$54,978.74	$3,436.17
Private	4	$30,515.00	$7,828.75
Public			
Class A	8	$13,215.00	$1,776.87
Others	3	$ 2,540.00	$ 846.66
Total	11	$15,755.00	$1,250.45
All Class A Colleges	20	$76,311.74	$3,665.58
All Other Colleges	11	$24,937.00	$2,267.00
Grand Total	31	$101,248.74	$3,266.08

The 11 public colleges reporting any appropriation for religious work listed a total of $15,755 budgeted for this purpose. This amounts to an average of $1,250.45 per institution. It should be borne in mind that doubtless the state institutions actually spend somewhat more than the figures indicate. Officials in some of these institutions do not feel free to make or to report any definite appropriations for religion.

Comparison of Class A college budgets with those of other institutions. The statistics show that, as compared with the other colleges, the Class A institutions budget considerably more for religious work than other colleges do. This difference is to be noted in both the church-related and the private institutions. The 20 Class A colleges budgeted $74,311.74, an average per college of $3,655.58, for religious work. The 11 Class B and unaccredited colleges appropriated a total of $34,937, an average of $2,667 per college. The difference is quite marked in the group of church-related colleges, where 8 Class A institutions budgeted more than $10,000 in excess of the amount of money appropriated for religious work by the same number of Class B or unaccredited schools. For the former the total budget was $32,381.34 and for the latter it was $22,397. It is also of interest to observe that the 8 Class A church-related colleges appropriated more than $19,000 in excess of what the 8 Class A public colleges budgeted. The 8 Class A church-related colleges budgeted an average of $4,071.46 per college, while the appropriations of the 8 Class A public institutions showed an average of $1,776.87 for each institution.

Comparison of present budget with that of previous years. The extent to which the colleges are appropriating more money for religious purposes now than in the past will be of interest. The question was raised as to whether the amount budgeted for religious work in 1940–41 represented more, less, or approximately the same sum appropriated in previous years. Twenty-seven colleges replied to this item. Of this number, 11 indicated that it was more than in previous years, while 14 replied that the amount budgeted for 1940–41 was about the same as in the past. It is significant to note that a larger percentage of public colleges than of either of the other two types appropriated more for religious work in 1940–41 than in previous years.

Distribution of religious budget. Twenty-nine colleges reported the way in which the budgetary provisions for religious work were distributed. The total amount budgeted by these institutions was $87,448.74, averaging $3,015.47 per institution. Reference to Table XI will reveal a summary of the total amounts budgeted for various purposes in those 29 colleges.

Ranking first in the size of appropriation is the amount for full-time instructors' salaries. Ten colleges reported a total of $32,017 distributed for this purpose, averaging $3,201.70 per college. By far the largest pro-

TABLE XI

SUMMARY TABLE SHOWING DISTRIBUTION OF BUDGETARY
PROVISIONS FOR RELIGIOUS WORK BY THE COLLEGE
ADMINISTRATIONS IN 29 INSTITUTIONS

Budgetary Item	Number of Colleges Reporting	Total Amount Budgeted	Average Amount per College
1. Full time salaries	10	$32,017.00	$3,201.70
2. Salary of Chaplain	12	23,505.00	1,958.75
3. Part-time salaries	10	11,612.00	1,161.20
4. Visiting ministers	21	5,140.00	244.76
5. Library books	14	1,521.00	108.65
6. Retreats	13	1,330.00	102.30
7. Religious Forums	8	1,165.63	145.70
8. Special facilities	9	1,097.00	121.88
9. Others	15	10,061.11	670.75
Total	29	$87,448.74	$3,015.47

portion of this sum was in the Class A colleges and all of the remainder was in the church-related and private schools. No state college reported any amount appropriated for full-time instruction in religion. Eight church colleges reported a total appropriation of $32,917 for full-time instruction, while 2 private institutions appropriated $8,000 for this purpose. In the individual reports, the salaries for full-time instruction in religion ranged from $1,200 to $4,000 a year. It is to be remembered that, while the average for the 10 colleges reporting full-time instructors' salaries is $3,201.70 each, in most of these institutions there are two or more full-time instructors in religion. It is clear that in these institutions the salary scale is relatively low.

The next largest appropriation was for salaries of the directors of religious life or chaplains, for which an average of $1,958.75 per college was appropriated. The average for the 8 Class A colleges was $2,067.50, and for the 4 remaining institutions it was $1,741.25. In some instances the salary figures given included perquisites in the form of house rent and did not represent actual cash outlay.

Salaries for part-time religious instruction ranked third in the amount of money appropriated, with 10 colleges budgeting an average of $1,161.20 each for this purpose. The one public institution in this group reported a budget of $1,600.

General status of teachers' salaries. The general inadequacy of salaries is one of the most important factors which affect the efficiency of Negro college teachers. Knox's study of 32 church-related colleges in 1931 showed that "the median salary of $1,511 annually paid instructors in the colleges studied is only 50 per cent of the minimum salary of $3,004 paid assistant professors in leading American colleges." [3] The discrepancies become more meaningful when comparisons are made between Negro and white teachers in the South. Figures recently compiled by the United States Office of Education,[4] based on the 3,935 white and 844 Negro teachers in 17 white and 17 Negro land-grant colleges located in as many states in the South, showed that median salaries of Negro teachers on the basis of 12 months ranged from $1,269 for instructors to $2,361 for deans. Median salaries for teachers in the white land-grant colleges in the same states ranged from $1,886 for instructors to $5,175 for deans. For full professors on the 9 months basis there was a difference of $1,827 in median salaries of white and Negro teachers.

These low incomes, of course, have a direct bearing on the quality of

3. Ellis O. Knox, "The Trend of Progress in the Light of New Educational Concepts in a Group of American Colleges Dominated by Religious Influences" (Ph.D. dissertation, University of Southern California, Los Angeles, 1931).

4. Maude Farr, *College Salaries, 1939–40*, Federal Security Agency, United States Office of Education, Circular No. 196 (Washington, 1940).

instruction which the teachers are able to give as well as on the morale of the teachers themselves. It means that the average Negro college teacher, being compelled to abide by a living standard higher than his salary comfortably permits, is unable to provide himself conveniently with many of the accoutrements of his professional status such as journals, books, attendance at professional meetings, and summer-school study. The threat of insecurity tends to hamper the development and maintenance of high morale, without which no adequate teaching program can be carried on. Davis describes the situation tersely:

Boldly stated—he [the Negro professor] is criminally underpaid. Having slaved at the most menial and humiliating work for a period of from five to ten years in order to get his degrees from a high-priced northern university, he comes out finally with a body often impaired in health and practically always a large debt to pay—money which he has had to borrow to supplement that which he has so painfully earned. He is then ready to go to work; and if he is fortunate enough to get a position he can look forward to an annual salary of less than *two thousand dollars a year*.[5]

Obviously, until Negro colleges are able to secure more adequate financial support and endowments this situation will continue.

Other appropriations for religion. Many of the colleges provided relatively small budgets for bringing in outside ministers or speakers. Several of the institutions made no budget provisions whatever for this purpose. Of the 29 institutions reporting on the distribution of the religious budgets, 21 reported a total of $5,140 set aside for visiting ministers. This is an average of $216.44 per college. In at least one instance where no indication was made of the distribution of the religious budget, the investigator knows that approximately $1,500 is annually set aside for this purpose. At this institution some of the outstanding ministers in the country are brought to the campus for the Sunday morning worship services.

It is at the point of contacts with outside ministers and other speakers that many students reap the greatest benefit from the chapel programs. As will be pointed out later, some of the students have stated positively that the most prevalent benefits from the chapel exercises are due to such contacts. That the colleges as a whole need to do more in this area than is being done at present is clear from the above figures.

According to the reports given, it is apparent that some of the schools have sensed the need for sponsoring religious retreats or conferences for small groups of students. Thirteen institutions reported budgeting a total of $1,330 for such exercises, or $102.30 per college. These opportunities for groups of student leaders and others interested in the relation of re-

5. A. P. Davis, "The Negro Professor," *The Crisis*, XLIII (April, 1938), 103.

ligion to life in general and to the life on the campus in particular constitute some of the best means for mediating religion in higher education.
At this point the Class B or unaccredited colleges are doing considerably
more than are the Class A institutions. The average budget for this item
in the former was $120 per college, while that for the Class A colleges
was $51.65 for each institution.

Religious forums constitute another item for which the colleges are
making appropriations. Eight colleges replied that a total of $1,165.63,
an average of $145.70, was appropriated for this purpose.

College officials were asked to what extent they appropriated money for
certain special facilities used in connection with religious work. Nine of
the institutions reported a total of $1,097, averaging $121.88, for this
part of the provisions for religion. Such facilities included principally the
equipment and upkeep of special rooms set aside for religious organizations.

A final item for which specific appropriations were listed is that of
library books. Fourteen schools budgeted an aggregate of $1,525, an aver-
age of $108.92 each. Here again the appropriations by the Class B and
unaccredited institutions were slightly more than those by the Class A
schools. Seven of the former budgeted an average of $117.14 for library
books in religion as compared with 7 Class A schools which appropriated
an average of $100.78 for the same purpose.

Budgets of student religious organizations. The total picture of the
financial provisions for religious work on the campus will be more nearly
complete with some consideration of the amount of money budgeted by
the voluntary student religious organizations themselves. Statistics were
available from a total of 50 organizations in 28 colleges. Twenty-one of
these organizations were in church-related schools, 5 were in private
schools, while 24 were in public institutions. Table XII exhibits the data
regarding the total budget provisions for the school year 1940–41 by the
50 organizations. The statistics are arranged according to type and
accreditation of college.

The 50 student religious organizations in 28 colleges reported a total
amount of $9,138.70 budgeted for 1940–41, an average of $182.77 for
each organization reporting. The larger percentage of this amount was
appropriated by organizations connected with the Student Christian
Movement, namely, the Y.M.C.A., the Y.W.C.A., and coeducational Student Christian Associations. Of course these organizations outnumber
by two to one the other types of student religious groups, whose total
budget was $531, an average of $59 each. When the budgets for all the
student religious organizations are compared by accreditation of college,
it is clear that here as in other instances the Class A colleges are able to
provide proportionally more funds for religious work than the other in-

TABLE XII

BUDGETS OF 50 STUDENT RELIGIOUS ORGANIZATIONS IN 28 COLLEGES

1940–41

TYPE OF ORGANIZATION

Type of Institution	No.	Y.M.C.A.	No.	Y.W.C.A.	No.	S.C.A.	No.	Misc.	No.	Totals by Type of College	Average per College
Church-related											
Class A	2	$ 813.20	5	$1,090.00	–	$ –	4	$240.00	11	$2,143.20	$194.03
Others	3	650.00	3	655.00	1	50.00	3	101.00	10	1,456.00	145.60
Private	2	1,250.00	1	300.00	2	747.00	–	–	5	2,297.50	459.50
Public											
Class A	7	925.00	8	1,487.00	1	125.00	2	190.00	18	2,727.00	151.50
Others	4	437.50	2	77.50	–	–	–	–	6	515.00	85.50
Totals by Organizations	18	$4,075.70	19	$3,609.50	4	$922.00	9	$531.00	50	$9,138.70	$182.77

stitutions are able to do. Thirty-four student religious organizations in Class A institutions budgeted a total of $7,167.70, an average of $210.81 each. At the same time, 16 such groups in Class B or unaccredited colleges budgeted a total of $1,971, averaging $123.18 per organization.

The student religious organizations in the state colleges budgeted somewhat less than those in the church-related institutions. Twenty-four such groups in tax-supported colleges appropriated an average of $135.08, as compared with 21 organizations in church-related colleges which budgeted an average per society of $171.39. For the 5 student religious organizations in private institutions there was a total budget of $2,297.50, which amounts to $459.50 per college. It is striking that the amount of money budgeted in private institutions by both the college administrations and voluntary student religious organizations is considerably higher than it is in the church-related and public colleges.

Of the 44 colleges reporting, 36 had a Y.M.C.A. Budgets for only half of these were listed, however. These 18 Y.M.C.A.'s reported a total budget for 1940–41 of $4,075.70, an average of $226.37 per school. The amounts for the individual organizations ranged from $25 to $900 for the year.

The 19 Y.W.C.A. groups for which figures are available listed a total budget of $3,607.53, an average of $189.85 for each organization. In addition, the 4 coeducational Student Christian Associations reported a total appropriation of $922.50. This is an average of $230.62 per school.

The foregoing statistics concerning the budgets of the student religious organizations suggest that these groups are hardly able to provide many of the activities which require any considerable expenditure of funds. The average student religious organization stands woefully in need of larger funds with which to carry on a successful program.

Budget sources of student religious organizations. Fifteen student religious organizations reported receiving 100 per cent of their budgets from student activities fees. Nine others reported receiving from 75 to 96 per cent of their income from this source. Two others reported receiving between 50 and 74 per cent of their yearly expenditures from student activities fees. Altogether, a total of 30 organizations were said to receive either all or part of their income from activities fees collected through the business office of the college.

Those organizations which receive all or at least the larger portion of their incomes from student activities fees are assured of having resources more adequate than other groups. Yet, as pointed out in previous discussion, there is sometimes a definite disadvantage in this practice. It virtually amounts to collection of the budget by force and is distasteful for those students whose real interests may not be with the religious group. Moreover, it is often true that, in those instances where the budgets are assured, the students themselves lose some of the values in the development of incentive, initiative, and loyalty which derive from the efforts to make one's organization successful or outstanding. Certainly much of the interest students demonstrate in their Greek-letter societies stems from the hard work and sacrifices which many of them have to put forth in order to make the organizations successful. It cannot be denied, therefore, that there is almost inevitably some loss sustained when the student religious organizations receive their income without having to put forth any special efforts for it.

Other sources from which student religious organizations receive their support are membership fees, faculty and student contributions, and occasional outright contributions from the college budget.

Contributions of student organizations to national movements. The amount of money the students contribute through their religious organizations to national student movements will be a partial index to their interests in these movements as well as to their ability or financial possibilities for sharing in the support of the national work. Statistics were secured from 45 student religious organizations concerning their contributions to the following national and international movements: the Y.M.C.A., the Y.W.C.A., the World Student Christian Federation, and the Far Eastern Student Emergency Fund (now the World Student Service Fund).

The 46 organizations made appropriations in their budgets to these movements totaling $1,165.25, an average of $25.35 for each one. On the basis of the average amount of each budget, this means that close to 14 per cent of the total budget was for contributions to national movements. The total number of contributions was 81 in all, making an average donation of $14.27 for each one.

The Y.M.C.A. and the Y.W.C.A. are respectively the national movements to which the largest contributions are given. Twenty-one proposed contributions to the Y.M.C.A. averaged $20.80 each, while 24 appropriations for the Y.W.C.A. averaged $17.04 each. The World Student Christian Federation, representing the total Student Christian Movement in its international ramifications, was to have received during the school year 1940–41 a total of $168.50 from 20 student religious organizations, an average contribution of $8.44 for each organization. The other organization for which budget provisions were made was the Far Eastern Student Emergency Fund. Fifteen organizations budgeted a total of $149.95 to this fund or an average of $9.93 for each group.

The student organizations reported here can be said to have given some thought to the national student movements from which they stem. The organizations making contributions to the national movements were the Y.M.C.A., the Y.W.C.A., and the coeducational Student Christian Associations, of which there were a total of 81 found in 44 colleges. Since we have statistics from only 55 per cent of these organizations indicating some contribution to one or more of the national movements, it is apparent that a fairly large proportion of these groups for some reason are failing to participate in the financial support of these larger groups. Much of this is to be attributed to the limited budgets upon which many of these organizations operate. But it is also true that many of them do not feel the urge deeply enough to make contributions the immediate results of which they do not at once recognize in their own organization. In addition to this, the limitations of personnel of the national staffs of the Student Christian Associations have made it a task of no small proportions for personal visitations to be made with any degree of regularity to the individual colleges. Such visitations are indispensable in creating and maintaining the sense of unity or of integration with a national movement of which the local association is a part. That this sense of participation in a national or world movement is most desirable cannot be denied. It will be one means of helping Negro students to transcend much of the feeling of not "belonging" which is likely to beset them, due to the limitations generally felt because of systematic discriminations to which they are subjected.

IX

UPPERCLASSMAN OPINION ON THE RELIGIOUS LIFE OF THE CAMPUS

WHAT students themselves think of the religious life and program of the college is of significance in any study of religion in higher education. It has already been shown, however, that there is no unanimity on this subject. There are some teachers who are of the opinion that the average college student is prepared neither emotionally, intellectually, nor from the point of view of personal experience adequately to estimate the significance of religion, either for himself or for the life of the college as a whole. But in spite of this distrust of student opinion it is safe to conclude that whatever the student thinks or feels about the significance of the religious program on the campus does have meaning and value. College administrators are generally prone to respect students' reactions to various other aspects of the programs of their institutions. The students' opinions concerning the religious life of the college should, therefore, carry some weight.

Upon the above assumption an attempt was made to gather the judgments of students as to their attitudes toward religion as they have observed it during the first one or two years of their college experience. A schedule of questions was prepared, designed to exhibit in specific as well as in general ways what students are thinking and saying regarding religion on their campuses. Because the students of junior and senior college classifications have had more experience in college and are more mature by virtue of relative chronological and scholastic advancement as compared with freshmen and sophomores, the investigation was confined to the students of these two upper classes.[1]

The 1,345 students included in this study were fairly typical of the upperclassmen in Negro colleges as a whole. In the first place, the 33 institutions represented in the study are among the outstanding colleges offering a standard four-year curriculum. More than 63 per cent were accredited Class A, and the geographical distribution of the colleges covers 16 states and the District of Columbia. Again, represented among

---

1. A total of 1,345 replies from 33 institutions, of which 21 were Class A, was used in the final tabulations, an average of approximately 41 questionnaires per college. It is to be noted that 13 of the colleges were church-related, 5 were private, and 15 were public. Four hundred twenty-seven, or 32 per cent, of the replies came from church-related colleges; 293, 22 per cent, were from private colleges; and 624, 46 per cent, came from public institutions.

the institutions were 20 per cent of the church-related, 44 per cent of the private, and 48 per cent of the public colleges for Negroes. The proportion of men and women students was not much different from the proportion of men and women in the colleges as a whole; and, finally, as Table XIII indicates, 93 per cent of the students responding were church members. These figures indicate that the opinions of the students of this study should reflect the attitudes of the typical upperclassmen in the representative colleges for Negroes.

TABLE XIII

DENOMINATIONAL AFFILIATION OF 1,345 STUDENTS
IN 33 COLLEGES

| | | | Type of College | |
Denomination		Total	Church-related	Private	Public
Baptists		591	204	105	282
Methodists		402			
Methodist	255		64	58	133
A.M.E.	95		30	23	42
C.M.E.	30		15	4	11
A.M.E.Z	22		7	5	11
Presbyterian		66	32	16	18
Catholic		57	15	11	31
Episcopal		46	13	13	20
Congregational-Christian		32	11	9	12
Christian Scientist		3	–	3	–
Church of God		3	1	–	2
Lutheran		3	–	1	2
Other denominations		19	7	5	7
Total church members		1,222			
Non-church		95	36	17	19
No answer		28			
Total		1,345			

Church attendance and activities of students. It appears evident that, taken as a whole, the students of this study attend church and engage in church activities fairly regularly when at home. More than 700 of the 1,345 students reported that they engaged in regular Sunday-school work, while 445 reported that they participated in the work of some Christian youth organization such as the Baptist Young People's Union, the Epworth League, or the Christian Endeavor Society.

Moreover, the results of the study show that the Negro college student does not altogether neglect church attendance when at home. Practically 50 per cent of the respondents said that they attended church every Sunday when at home, while another 25 per cent said that they attended church at least 3 Sundays per month. Seventy-five per cent of the students, therefore, asserted that they attended church with a remarkable degree of regularity. Again, 17 per cent of the students asserted that they attended church as often as twice a month. A relatively small number indicated that they attended church less than 12 Sundays a year and a few affirmed that they never attended church.

A criticism has sometimes been made that the college educates students away from the church. If the students are accurate in the statements made in this questionnaire, it would appear that, should a negative attitude with respect to church-going result from college education, it is not very noticeable before the end of the college experience. One is safe in saying, therefore, that Negro college students in general do not neglect the church. Here is a basis for much more optimism than has often been felt with regard to the responsiveness of college youth toward religion and the church. Other students of the problem have found similar results.[2]

Attitudes of students toward courses in religion. The question of offering courses in religion has been one of the important issues in higher education in recent years. What students think of courses in religion to which they have been exposed is of value in estimating the effect of the college program at this point. In response to the request, "If you are taking or have taken college courses in religious subjects, check the word which best describes your estimate of these courses: fascinating, interesting, not very stimulating, dull," replies were made by 719 students or 53 per cent of the total number of respondents.

As many as 8 per cent of the students replying to this question said that their courses in religion were "fascinating," while a surprisingly large number, 77 per cent, said that they found their religious courses "interesting." It should be observed here, however, that while the word "interesting" does not give as definite a clue to the real reaction of the students as is desirable it does give some indication of a favorable response to the academic study of religion. The large number of students checking this reaction implies further that the college teachers of religion were, as a whole, stimulating. Only 10 per cent of the students indicated

2. "Negro college students are motivated by high ideals. This is revealed by the reasons given for attending the college of their choice; reasons given for their choice of occupation; types of hobbies in which they are predominantly interested; and their affiliation with religious interests. . . . Nearly four-fifths of these students attended church and Sunday School regularly during their high school career and only 0.39 per cent said that they did not attend church at all. Ninety-five per cent of the students claimed membership in a church. This fact should be of special import to Negro colleges in stimulating them to nurture and preserve the high ideals of students." Ambrose Caliver, *A Background Study of Negro College Students*, United States Office of Education Bulletin, 1933, No. 8 (Washington, United States Government Printing Office, 1933), p. 108.

that their courses were "not very stimulating" and 5 per cent checked the word "dull" as descriptive of their reaction. If we should take the total number of students who checked either "fascinating" or "interesting," we would find that 85 per cent have a positively favorable attitude to the study of religion, while at the same time 15 per cent have an unfavorable attitude.

Estimate of students' attitudes toward religion. A striking situation is revealed in the responses to the question regarding the students' attitudes toward religion. In answer to the request, "Please give your estimate of your fellow students as a whole toward religion: interested, indifferent, hostile," 35 per cent checked the word "interested," 59 per cent checked the word "indifferent," and 6 per cent checked the word "hostile."

In the light of the statistics already given concerning church membership and attendance of college students when at home, the question naturally arises as to why it is that, while 93 per cent of the students were church members and more than 90 per cent attended church from twice a month to every Sunday a month, only 35 per cent felt that their fellow students were interested in religion. Also of significance in the answer to this item is the fact that so large a proportion of students, 59 per cent, seemed to be of the opinion that their fellow students had no interest in religion. Sixty-two per cent of the men and 56 per cent of the women gave this estimate. Whatever the concept of religion which the students had in mind as they gave these estimates, the conclusion is evident that college youth do not, as a whole, think of each other as being interested in religion.

In Mays' study of the religious attitudes of Negro students a similar situation was found. He reported that

The religious attitude which students express for themselves is slightly different from that which they express for their fellow students. This is shown by the fact that 63 per cent of 400 students listed religion as one of the factors that influence their life most as over against a smaller percentage, 57 per cent, who expressed the belief that religion was a vital influence in the life of the students and 40 per cent who said that it was not a vital influence. This fact is further revealed in the constructive answers given to the question, what does religion mean to you, as contrasted with the critical answers given to the question dealing with the mind of youth in religion. As youth observes the activities of his fellow students, he is inclined to feel that they are not religious. But when he thinks of his own religion and speaks for himself, he is more likely to speak positively about it.[3]

3. Report of the Conference of College Religious Workers, Fisk University, Nashville, Tennessee, March 7–10, 1929, p. 8.

The small number of students who said that their fellow students were hostile to religion is in line with the results of the faculty estimates of students' hostility to religion as given in the conferences reported in Chapter III. As was indicated there, no faculty group among the ones visited reported having any students positively hostile to religion or definitely atheistic. It may be concluded that the average Negro college student is not imbued with any spirit of active opposition to religion.

Attitude toward compulsory chapel. In view of the place which chapel exercises hold in the life of the college program, an attempt was made to discover how the students estimate their value. Several different answers were given to the following question, "What benefits do you see in the chapel exercises on your campus?" In each case the benefit upon which major stress was placed was counted in the tabulation. Only 7 per cent of the students failed to answer this question. Table XIV shows the data on this item.

TABLE XIV

EVALUATION OF THE BENEFITS OF COLLEGE CHAPEL BY 1,345 STUDENTS IN 33 COLLEGES ARRANGED BY TYPE OF COLLEGE

Benefits	Total	Type of College Church-related	Private	Public
1. Worship and the development of the devotional life	476	160	114	202
2. Instruction in Bible and culture	202	45	48	109
3. Broadening contact with others	162	40	46	76
4. Cultivation of the moral life	61	18	8	35
5. Fellowship and unity	39	14	7	18
6. Development of student leadership	35	13	5	17
7. Break in daily routine	10	–	6	4
8. Social vision	5	3	–	2
9. Other benefits	19	9	1	9
10. Very little benefits	136	53	22	61
11. No benefits	101	37	21	43
12. No answer	99	36	15	48
Total	1,345	428	293	624

A rather sizable minority, 17.5 per cent, frankly stated that they saw little or no benefit in the chapel exercises. While the majority of this group expressed their reaction simply, there were others who took occasion to emphasize their objections in such expressions as "absolutely none," "none, except to give the monitors a job," and "no benefits except to receive announcements."

It is of significance to note, however, that as many as 80 per cent of the students did see some benefits in the chapel programs, the emphases being placed predominantly upon such values as worship and the development of the devotional life, instruction in Bible and general culture, and broadening contact with others. Typical of some of the reactions of students in regard to the benefits of worship to be found in chapel programs are the following: "It is good to be able to hear inspiring addresses and to listen to sacred music each day." "Chapel services keep us next to the religious side of life." "Chapel programs aid us in starting the day off right." Some of the students felt that the programs enabled them to "gain knowledge about various aspects of life, aspects of art and various opinions about religion and society."

One important feature of chapel programs, as seen from the students' point of view, is that they provide opportunity for young people to become acquainted with a variety of personalities other than those on the campus. One student said, for example, that "the speakers often talk on their experiences, world travel, current events or personal ideas." Another asserted that, through "visiting ministers, we are exposed to a variety of opinions, ideas and theories."

It is of interest to observe that some of the respondents recognized in the chapel programs an opportunity for the development of student leadership. Others suggested that the chapel services presented an opportunity to enjoy a break in the daily routine of the campus. Still another value given by a very few students was that of social vision. It is certainly at this point that the college may assist its students in breaking down some of the prejudices that have their origin in the caste system.

There is a noticeable difference between the appreciation of students in the private college for the chapel programs and the appreciation expressed by students in church-related and public institutions. As many as 21 per cent of the students in the church-related and 19 per cent in the public colleges saw little or no benefits in the chapel exercises. On the other hand, only 14 per cent of the students in the private institutions expressed this particular attitude. One explanation for this is probably that compulsory attendance is more prevalent in the church-related colleges than in the private ones. Moreover, it may be that the chapel exercises in the church-related institutions are less carefully planned than are those in the other types of colleges. As a matter of fact, a somewhat larger percentage of students in church-related colleges than in other types of institutions criticized the chapel exercises on the grounds of their being monotonous and poorly planned. In addition to this, the figures for the budget provisions for religious work indicate that more money is spent by private institutions for this purpose than by those colleges under other types of control, thus making it possible for the private schools to enrich their offerings in religious services to a greater extent than the other schools are able to do.

The criticisms of college chapel. Besides offering an opportunity for students to state the benefits they saw in college chapel, the privilege was also given them to express their criticisms of these services. Obviously the criticisms of students at this point should have an important significance for those who are interested in the religious program of the college.

A much larger percentage of students answered the item providing for statements of the benefits of chapel than the item providing for the criticisms of chapel. Whereas there were 7 per cent who failed to answer the former question, 26 per cent failed to state any criticisms of the chapel services. This fact is quite suggestive. It may be that the students are not as critical of the chapel programs as they sometimes think they are or as is commonly believed, or they may be unable to put their objections to chapel into concrete expression. Or, again, it may simply be an indication of docility on the part of students failing to criticize the services.

A total of 13 per cent of the students stated that they had no criticisms to make of the chapel programs on their campuses, as seen in Table XV, on page 114. In the space provided for the expression of criticisms of chapel some of the students in this group simply wrote "none" or "no criticism to offer." Others took the occasion to point out some aspects of the chapel exercises which they appreciated.

The major criticisms which students made of the chapel services were at the points of their being poorly planned and monotonous, compulsory, having no appeal to student interests and need, and the presentations by ineffective speakers. Such criticisms of college chapel exercises are not new. The predominance of these reactions in this study shows, however, that those in positions of responsibility for chapel programs need still to give especial attention to seeing that no pains are spared in making the services consciously significant in the lives of students.

Ten per cent of the criticisms emphasized that the chapel programs were "too monotonous, a repetition," that "very little preparation is made for them," or that the services are "undiversified, too superficial, and the general tone is not conducive to volitional worship." On this point there has been considerable criticism on the part of students through the years. In the study by Mays to which reference has been made, the following conclusion was drawn: "Students complain that the religious programs are dry, dull and lack variety. Nine out of ten colleges make this criticism." [4]

4. *Ibid.*, p. 7.

TABLE XV

THE CRITICISMS OF COLLEGE CHAPEL BY 1,345 UPPERCLASS-
MEN IN 33 COLLEGES ARRANGED BY TYPE OF COLLEGE

Criticisms	Total	Type of College Church-related	Private	Public
1. No criticism to offer	175	51	47	77
2. Programs poorly planned, monotonous	141	52	20	69
3. Compulsory nature of service	130	43	39	48
4. No appeal to student interests and needs	102	29	22	51
5. Ineffective speakers and speeches	99	32	34	33
6. Services too frequent and too lengthy	89	36	14	39
7. Lack of religious atmosphere and materials	87	17	16	54
8. Lack of genuine interest on the part of the students and faculty	55	21	12	22
9. Too formal	42	10	8	24
10. Lack of student participation	17	5	7	5
11. Conflicting ideas set forth	3	1	–	2
12. Other criticisms	62	11	15	36
13. No answer	343	120	59	164
Total	1,345	428	293	624

Contrary to some of the opinion relative to the lack of variety in the services as expressed above, a small number of students, not more than four or five, expressed the view that the chapel services ought to be more uniform than they are. Such is the attitude of the student who asserted, "I feel that as different people conduct chapel they should try to have a uniform type of worship." It should also be pointed out that in any group of returns from the same institution, conflicting criticisms of the chapel exercises were expressed. Obviously, students have varying standards as to what constitutes a helpful chapel service.

Compulsory attendance has been generally considered the most common objection to the chapel programs on the part of students. As was pointed out in Chapter IV of this study, at least 86 per cent of all the Negro institutions studied required attendance at some form of chapel service. Out of the 43 colleges surveyed on this point, the proportion requiring compulsory attendance was about the same among the public institutions as among the church-related and private colleges.

Slightly less than 10 per cent of the students criticized the chapel programs on the ground that they were compulsory, saying in effect, as one student put it, that "compulsory attendance destroys the purpose of chapel talks. It inhibits rather than facilitates clear thinking." It appears to this investigator, however, that if the compulsory chapel programs were made more stimulating from the point of view of additional variety and more careful planning there would be much less objection to attendance on the part of students.

While slightly less than 10 per cent of the criticisms of chapel in this study were at the point of compulsion, Mays's conclusion from his investigation in 1929 was that "Almost all students are positively opposed to compulsory services for college students. They argue that forced services are ineffective; that college students are advanced enough to be placed on their own merit; that character is not developed through compulsion." [5]

The criticism that chapel programs do not appeal to student interest and needs, made by 8 per cent of the students, is of particular interest. Obviously, many of the subjects about which chapel speeches are made are much more important than the students often realize. The difficulty of making the important materials seem important to the students is a real one, due to the limitations involved in securing effective speakers for the vital subjects.

One of the significant findings of this study is that a few students criticized the chapel programs on the ground that they were lacking in religious atmosphere and materials. Between 6 and 7 per cent of the students emphasized this criticism. This fact supports the view that many of the college students are positively interested in religion and its values. Typical of the comments on this point are the following: "Chapel services are too often non-religious in character." "Chapel exercises are usually composed of announcements and less stress is placed upon the religious part." "The chapel services are too academic, therefore, not helpful as a spiritual stimulus." The majority of such comments come from state institutions where sometimes care is taken to avoid any tendency toward religious indoctrination and also where trained religious leadership is not always available. Nine per cent of the respondents in the state colleges made the criticism that the chapel services were lacking in religious elements. On the other hand, only 5 per cent of the students in private colleges and 3 per cent of those in church-related institutions made this criticism.

One conclusion to which the above reaction points is that too often the speakers in college chapel for some reason avoid making a religious em-

5. *Ibid.*

phasis in their talks. It is probable that this is sometimes done on the assumption that students would not be interested in a strictly religious address. It is true also that some speakers avoid speaking on religious themes because of a feeling of inadequacy in this field. In any case, it appears that religion is felt to be a definite need on the part of college students and that this need is being more adequately met by the church-related and private institutions than by the state colleges.

Attitudes of students toward the religious sincerity of the college administration and staff. The college that attempts to be religious will seek somehow to let its students see the principles of religion in operation in the various phases of its activities. If the students themselves do not see religious ideals implicit in their teachers, both in the personal lives of the instructors and in the conditions which are provided for the curricular and the extracurricular activities of the campus, they will be deprived of one of the most important potential educative forces in their college career. In view of this consideration, a simple question was raised designed to throw some light on how the students of this study felt toward the religious sincerity of their teachers. The question was: "Do you feel that, in general, the college administration and staff exemplify in their activities and responsibilities a genuine religious spirit?" The limitations of the phrasing of this question are readily admitted. Space was provided only for a categorical answer of "yes" or "no." Some opportunity could have been provided for students to express certain qualifications or gradations of religious sincerity on the part of teachers. In spite of these limitations, it is felt that the answers made to this question will be some useful index to how effectively the college is succeeding in its efforts to mediate religious and moral principles to its students through its own activities.

Forty-nine per cent of the students answered "yes" to the above question while 46 per cent answered "no," as shown in Table XVI. Five per

TABLE XVI

ATTITUDES OF 1,345 UPPERCLASSMEN TOWARD THE RELIGIOUS SINCERITY OF THE COLLEGE ADMINISTRATION AND STAFF IN 33 COLLEGES ARRANGED BY TYPE OF COLLEGE

| Response | Total | Type of College | | |
		Church-related	Private	Public
Yes	637	251	136	250
No	611	149	133	329
No answer	97	28	24	45
Total	1,345	428	293	624

cent failed to respond. In other words, it can be said that the majority of the students who answered the question feel that the colleges are religiously in earnest; yet the division of opinion here is quite close, and it is likely that if there had been 100 per cent response to the question the division of opinion would have been more nearly equal.

The percentage of replies favorable to the college faculties varied considerably when the individual colleges were studied. In some instances the replies were as much as 83 per cent favorable. In some other instances the replies were around 80 per cent negative. In still other instances there was fairly even balance in the replies. The net result of each type of reaction upon student morale and the shaping of attitudes is obviously profound.

The significance of this response is seen in that, while it is generally agreed that all of the college presidents believe in the value of religion for the educational process, less than 50 per cent of the students in the 33 colleges felt that the college administration and staff were themselves religious in their administrative relation to the students. The question may arise as to what the students had in mind by "genuine religious spirit" when they checked the answer to this question. The intention behind the statement of the question was to find out whether the students themselves were convinced that the faculty were honestly endeavoring to exemplify real religious sincerity. It is possible that some of the students may have interpreted the question in terms of the formal and overt expressions of religion such as conducting services of worship or in more-or-less active participation in such services. Yet, in spite of this possible inadequate understanding, the conclusion is drawn from a consideration of the responses as a whole that the interpretation of the question given by the students was generally in line with what was intended.

An important variation is to be seen in the replies to this item when they are compared according to the type of college from which they come. The figures show that in the church-related institutions the students predominantly feel that the administration and staff show a genuine religious spirit, while those in the private colleges are almost equally divided on the matter. On the other hand, the students in the public colleges are predominantly of the opinion that their administration and staff do not show a genuine religious spirit. Admitting that some of the students may have interpreted the question as suggested above, that is, in terms of the overt expression of religion in religious exercises, it is still striking that there is a marked contrast between the replies coming from the three types of colleges. This contrast suggests a real difference in the type of administrative relation to students which obtains in the church-related colleges and the public institutions. Fifty-nine per cent of the students in church-related colleges felt that the faculty demonstrated religion practically as compared with only 40 per cent of the students in public colleges. At the same time, 35 per cent of the students in the church-related colleges felt that the faculty did not show a genuine religious spirit, as compared with 52 per cent of the students in the public colleges. The answers for students in the private colleges were 46 per cent in the affirmative and 45 per cent in the negative.

One of the conclusions to which the figures just given may lead is that the presidents of the church-related colleges are more careful to select staff members along the line of their possible contributions to the religious life than are the presidents of private and public colleges. With the latter types of institutions the emphasis is primarily on the teachers' ability to handle their respective fields rather than upon the contribution they may make to religion on the campus. This is not to say that the teachers in the church-related colleges are not considered from the point of view of their scholarship and teaching ability but that the administrators of the church-related institutions, in response to the stated objectives of the college as well as in response to the demands imposed upon them by the denomination to which they are responsible, are of necessity more concerned about the religious qualifications of their instructors than are the presidents of other types of colleges.

Granted, however, that the teachers in the church-related colleges are rated more highly religiously than those in other institutions, the percentage of the affirmative answers to the question is not as high as possibly it should be. After all, only 59 per cent of the students in the church-related institutions expressed faith in the religious sincerity of their teachers. This number is relatively small in the light of the purposes of higher education in general and of the church-related college in particular. Unless the church-related institutions can be more convincing to the students at this point, they will hardly justify their claims.

Again, one may well raise the question as to what is the bearing on the objectives of any program of higher education, whether under church, private, or public control, of the students' failure to find genuine religious sincerity exemplified by their faculties. As has been pointed out, by far the large majority of students in all institutions for Negroes are church members. If upon coming to college they discover the absence of religious ideals in the faculty members themselves, it is not to be a matter of surprise if some students are influenced toward being less hospitable to religious motivation by the time they leave college.

The effectiveness of students active in religious work. In an attempt to find out how students evaluate their fellow students who work in the field of religion, the following question was raised, "Do the students who are most active in the religious program of the campus exert any real and practical influence upon the personal and moral life of the rest of the student body?" Fifty-five per cent of the replies were in the negative, while 38 per cent were in the affirmative. The remainder failed to respond.

Personal experience in several institutions, however, leads one to feel that this unfavorable reaction on the part of students is not representative of the real effectiveness of those of their number active in religious work. In some instances the student religious leaders are among the outstanding youth on the campus and are active not only in the Christian Associations but in many of the other organizations as well. Thus the real effectiveness of such students as religious influences on the campus may not be wholly recognized.

It should be said that much of the effectiveness of religious work on the campus will be determined by the extent to which such activity is able to attract competent student leadership. One of the conclusions which these figures suggest is that in many campus situations the religious organizations need a dynamic, motivating ideal that in itself will generate magnetic influence and command the attention and interest of college youth. Some of this dynamic is to be seen in certain nonreligious organizations. Greek-letter societies are almost always able to call forth deep loyalty and sacrifice and expenditure of energy on the part of students. When religious activities and organizations can meet these requirements the effectiveness of a religious program will be inevitable. Such agencies will then provide a cause to which the competent students will be able to give themselves unreservedly.

Outstanding religious and ethical problems faced by students. It is indispensable in planning any program of religion in higher education to have an understanding of the outstanding religious and moral problems students have. Obviously, the religious program of the campus must be designed to help meet the needs of students in these areas of their experience. For this reason what students themselves have to say rgarding their most significant problems will be a useful part of the study of religion on the campus. The question was put as follows, "What do you feel are the outstanding religious and ethical problems which students in your institution face in their college life?"

It is of significance to observe that of the 1,345 students of this study only 61 per cent replied to this question. This is quite likely to be attributed to the fact that many students are not able to give articulate expression to the problems they face. One would not deny that there are some students for whom life flows along rather smoothly, presenting no conflicts or issues perplexing to their thinking. In fact, one or two undergraduates plainly said that students were not interested enough to have any problems. Yet this estimate is hardly typical. Most persons acquainted with the psychology of adolescence would agree that it is common for youth of college age to be perplexed with problems of various kinds.

The largest percentage of replies to this question included problems related to some type of religious adjustment or thought, as Table XVII shows. Slightly more than 26 per cent of the students responding to this item listed problems that can be classified under this general category. In the tabulation of the returns, these replies were listed under the following heads: "changes and readjustments in religious and moral outlook," "theological problems," and "understanding the significance of religion and the church." For some students, to use the language of one of them, "the existence of God is a question in most minds." Others felt the major problem to be "the disregard of religion—tendency toward unbelief."

TABLE XVII

OUTSTANDING RELIGIOUS AND ETHICAL PROBLEMS LISTED BY STUDENTS IN 33 COLLEGES ARRANGED BY SEX

Problems	Total	Percentage *	Men	Women
1. Personal morality	192	23.2	95	97
2. Theological problems	105	12.7	58	47
3. Understanding the significance of religion	72	8.7	31	41
4. Neglect of the spiritual life	68	8.2	20	48
5. Compulsory chapel and church attendance	56	6.8	22	34
6. Social morality	42	5.1	18	24
7. Changes and readjustments in religious and moral outlook	42	5.1	18	24
8. Getting along with one's fellows	35	4.3	14	21
9. Maintaining inner integrity and control	33	4.0	19	14
10. Adjustment to new environment	28	3.4	14	14
11. Denominational differences	27	3.4	11	16
12. Relation between science and religion	23	2.8	7	16
13. Relation of religion to social problems	18	2.2	9	9
14. Desire for spiritual and moral uplift	15	1.8	6	9
15. Undesirable recreation	7	.8	4	3
16. Racial adjustment	5	.6	2	3
17. Other problems	57	6.9	27	30
18. No answer	520		179	341
Total	1,345		554	791

* The percentages are based on the 825 students who actually listed problems.

In regard to the more general problem of understanding the significance of religion and the church, it is clear that this is one of the important aspects of students' religious difficulties. Some students pointed out the major problem to be "finding out what religion is; knowing the function of it in our lives"; "the problem of students trying to find themselves among various philosophies"; and the fact that "what students are taught in college is sometimes different from what they learn at home, thus causing their ideas to change."

Yet, in spite of this sizable group, 26 per cent, expressing difficulties in the area of religious adjustment and interpretation, it is true that the majority of students are not atheistically inclined; neither can it be said that they are positively agnostic. Instead, the temper of the comments in general expresses uncertainty or questioning marked by a sincere attempt to discover the solution to the problems mentioned. The statistics here are in line with a comment made by one of the college presidents to which reference was made earlier; that is, that college students have "an unsatisfied yearning for religion."

Incidentally, the findings made by Bond in a study of the religious attitudes of 500 students in a small college are singularly similar at this point. Although Bond concluded that the students of his study are not concerned very much about theological problems, he asserts that there was "evident desire for reality in religious faith" and that they were "sincerely, if not intelligently religious," accepting the "time-honored values" such as "church, Christian association, Bible, prayer, belief in immortality, and Jesus." [6]

Nearly 13 per cent of the respondents of the present study listed problems in the area of personal morality. That students have always been keenly interested in problems of right and wrong has long been recognized. The transition from school to college is accompanied quite often by the problems incident to changing from parental or home authority to the somewhat less restrained life of the college community. In many instances students are not prepared for this new freedom. The contact with fellow students or faculty members of moral ideals different from their own or their parents' brings some acute problems of adjustment with respect to the meaning of right and wrong. Some of the problems listed in this area were "the problem of cheating," "the problem of controlling yourself when you are away from home," "the moral attitude toward life; what is wrong and why," and "honesty and loyalty to ideals."

The results here give rise to the conclusion that in general the students of this group are sincerely concerned about personal moral problems and

6. C. H. Bond, *A Study of the Religious Attitudes of 500 College Students* (New York, Bucknell University and the Board of Education of the Northern Baptist Convention, 1939), p. 24.

the relation of religion thereto. Such problems are common to youth regardless of race. Especially are these problems perplexing to students in an age when, for society in general, moral standards and ideals are in a state of flux. Unless the student is fairly well adjusted when he comes to college, the so-called "acids of modernity," combined with the normal problems of readjustment to new ideas he is likely to meet in college, will produce a period of moral uncertainty on his part.

Experiences that have hindered the development of students' religious faith. The outstanding religious and ethical problems which students face in their college life constitute some of the background of the experiences which hinder the development of their religious faith. A comparison shows a strong correlation between the religious and ethical problem area and the experiences that hinder religious faith. As stated in the questionnaire, the question was, "What experiences have you found to be a hindrance to your religious faith?"

A rather large variety of experiences was listed in response to this item, although only 61 per cent of the students provided data on this question. As in the case of the students' statements of the problems they face, it is quite likely that the hindering experiences were there but that a large percentage of students were unable to give satisfactory expression to them. A comparison between Table XVII and Table XVIII will show that the percentage of students failing to answer this item is the same as the number failing to respond to the question regarding problems students face.

At the outset it is noteworthy that slightly more than 25 per cent of the students giving data here stated definitely that they had no experiences hindering to their religious faith. The students of this group constitute the largest number answering in any one category listed and this number is eight points higher in percentage than the next highest group. Is it that these students' world, personal and social, has been so sheltered that they have had no hindering religious experiences or is it that they have been so well adjusted all along that they have weathered every possible attack on religious faith that has occurred to them in normal living? Both of these alternatives are doubtless applicable in a number of cases. But there is a third explanation which will probably take precedence over the two just mentioned. The theological background from which most Negro students come is relatively conservative and otherworldly. This would mean that religion is frequently interpreted rather narrowly by them; that is, they do not always see the relevance of some of the problems of thought, or even of social and personal problems, to religion. If this is the case, we have a type of religious adjustment which arises from spiritual shortsightedness rather than profound spiritual vision.

The fact that the largest number of hindering experiences listed by students relates to general problems of religious thought indicates the

TABLE XVIII

EXPERIENCES THAT HAVE HINDERED THE DEVELOPMENT
OF STUDENTS' FAITH

Hindering Experiences	Total	Percentage *	Men	Women
1. None	208	25.3	95	113
2. Influence of college courses	143	17.4	58	85
3. Problem of religious thought	100	12.2	44	56
4. Immorality of supposedly religious people	69	8.4	49	20
5. Influence of fellow students	49	6.0	26	23
6. Required chapel or religious courses	30	3.7	15	15
7. Scepticism on part of others	29	3.5	16	13
8. Religious frustration	26	3.2	13	13
9. Personal moral problems	19	2.3	13	6
10. Problem of recreation	19	2.3	4	15
11. Inadequacy of leaders in college of community	15	1.8	9	6
12. Influence of teachers	14	1.7	9	5
13. Adjustment to campus environment	14	1.7	8	6
14. Problems of race	14	1.7	7	7
15. Problem of practical social religion	13	1.6	3	10
16. Sunday work or play	12	1.5	6	6
17. Inadequacy of college provisions	9	1.1	2	7
18. Economic inequalities	6	.7	3	3
19. Religious orthodoxy	6	.7	4	2
20. Others	26	3.2	13	13
21. No answer	524		157	367
Total	1,345		554	791

* The percentages are based on the 821 students who actually listed hindering experiences.

difficulties involved in the transition from parental and home-church religious influences to those characteristic of the college community. Over 17 per cent of the students listed problems in these areas. The students must become adjusted to the new way of facing facts through the scientific method. Moreover, there is a correlation here between problems of religious thought as outstanding for students and problems of religious thought as experiences that hinder the development of the religious life. Experiences under this general heading were listed separately. Twelve per cent of the students replying listed as hindering experiences some problems dealing directly with religious thought, including such difficulties as "differences of opinion encountered in meeting students of different denominations other than mine," "the seeming invariable triumph of wrong over right," "contradictions in the Bible, and the hostility toward religion in general by individuals," and "the conflicts arising from the study of religion and science."

The influence of college courses is to be observed in the expressions of students at this point. Some of the courses listed as hindering the development of the religious life were even in the field of religion, as well as psychology and the natural sciences. As many as 17.5 per cent of the students responding to this item attributed experiences hindering religious faith to courses taken in college. For the student who is endeavoring sincerely to be religious, the problems in the area of the logical validation of religion are acute. Certainly the college cannot be too careful in endeavoring to make the provisions necessary for helping the undergraduate through the period of religious uncertainty which is likely to come in the life of every thoughtful student.

That students are vitally affected by the moral and spiritual life of their adult leaders is clear from the fact that a fairly large group mentioned the immorality of supposedly religious leaders and the inadequacy of leaders in the college or community as experiences that hindered their religious faith. According to some of the statements made in this connection, many of the students feel very keenly at this point. In reference to this one student, for example, said, "People who are preaching the faith are not living up to it." Another affirmed that difficulty was felt because of the "bigotry, hypocrisy and racial and color discriminations in the church itself." Still another type of reaction is that of the student who said that "most speakers 'talk through their hats.' They do not say what they really feel or mean." This is one of the most serious of the statements made by students regarding hindrances to religious faith. Although the percentage of times this criticism was mentioned is relatively small when compared with the other hindering experiences, it is nevertheless true that religious leaders must examine with humility the criticisms made against their moral and spiritual life, for it is often through the ideal of a worthy life that religion is transmitted to others and particularly to youth.

A few students said that required attendance at chapel or in courses in religion constituted experiences that hindered religious faith. Where such students belong to faiths or denominations different from those dominant in the religious services or in the class, it is easy to see that compulsory attendance would present a problem.

Other students indicated some aspect of religious frustration as hindering them spiritually. The frustrations were largely those arising from inability to attend the church of their choice or from being unable to attend church at all or as often as they desired. Unwholesome recreation was also mentioned by a few students. Again, the problems incident to racial discrimination and economic inequalities were mentioned but not as often as one might have thought. Here again the explanation is probably due to the fact that for many students these problems are not thought of as having close relation to one's religious faith because of the otherworldly presuppositions dominant in much conservative religious dogma.

These statistics show once more the general religious sincerity to be found among college youth. The statements are for the most part indicative of the idealism that is characteristic of adolescence. Certainly the college may well study how it may meet the intellectual and spiritual problems of its students with increasing facility and effectiveness.

Available college resources for help in solving students' personal problems. Having attempted to find out the problems which students face in their college experience, an effort was made to find out to what extent, in the students' own opinion, the college was providing agencies or individuals for help in the solution of their personal problems. The statement of the question was as follows: "What forces in your college are available to the students for help in solution of their personal problems?" Eighty-one per cent of the students answered this item.

Eight per cent of the 1,345 students stated that there were no forces for help available in their colleges. The distribution of this number by type of college shows that the largest percentage is to be found in the church-related institutions, as shown in Table XIX, on page 126. Ten per cent of the 428 students in the church-affiliated colleges and 7 per cent in the private and public colleges said that there were no available resources in their colleges for help in solving personal problems.

Why, one may inquire, do 8 per cent of the students of this study say positively that there are no forces in their colleges for help in solving personal problems? Since these students are scattered among the 33 colleges of this study rather than located in just a few institutions, it is likely that for them either there was no recognition of available resources or those resources available were considered ineffective by the students. In view of the fact that the majority of the students were able to list resources of various kinds, the second of these explanations is the more probable one.

Of the number of forces actually listed, the largest group was that of faculty advisers. These were not necessarily faculty members with the official title of "Adviser" but were simply members of the staff whom the students considered as helpful in an advisory capacity in the area of personal problems. The majority of other forces mentioned were, of course, faculty members.

TABLE XIX

AVAILABLE COLLEGE RESOURCES FOR HELP IN SOLVING
PERSONAL PROBLEMS AS LISTED BY 1,345 UPPERCLASS-
MEN IN 33 COLLEGES ARRANGED BY TYPE OF COLLEGE

			Type of College	
Resources Available	Total	Church-related	Private	Public
1. None	110	45	22	43
2. Faculty advisers	237	81	42	114
3. Personnel counselors	168	64	19	85
4. Dean of men	155	48	49	58
5. College minister	84	6	44	34
6. The Y.M.C.A.	70	20	12	38
7. Academic deans	35	6	12	17
8. Student council	33	7	7	19
9. Instructors in religion	28	19	1	8
10. Religious exercises	24	4	4	16
11. Dean of women	23	3	10	10
12. Student advisers	22	7	6	9
13. The Y.W.C.A.	20	8	2	10
14. The president	13	6	4	3
15. Courses in religion	13	8	1	4
16. Library books	11	3	1	7
17. House directors	10	3	4	3
18. Friends	7	1	—	6
19. Others	33	10	6	17
20. No answer	249	79	47	123
Total	1,345	428	293	624

Among the faculty groups mentioned most frequently as helpful resources were the deans of men, who were listed by 155 students. Some variation is observed when the returns are compared according to type of college. More students in private colleges than in church-related and public institutions mentioned the dean of men as a helpful counseling resource. The percentages were 17, 11, and 9, respectively. The explanation of this is doubtless that in the private colleges much more emphasis is put upon the dean of men as an advisory officer than in the other colleges. It is striking to note also that almost as large a proportion of women students mentioned the dean of men as did the men students. Thirteen per cent of the men and 10 per cent of the women students listed the dean of men. The influence of this officer is felt by both sexes, in the classroom as well as through his regular duties on the campus. It is also of interest to note that, while 12 per cent of the students listed the dean of men as a helpful resource in solving personal problems, only .7 per cent mentioned the dean of women. It appears that the deans of women, who are to be found in almost every coeducational and women's college, are not making themselves felt as effectively as are the deans of men.

Of more than ordinary interest is that 5 per cent of the students mentioned the Young Men's Christian Association on their campuses as a helpful resource in solving personal problems. In addition, 4 per cent of the students listed the Young Women's Christian Association and the Student Council. One may conclude from this study that in spite of the weaknesses of the student organizations these agencies constitute some of the helpful resources in the colleges for the personal adjustment of students. The active participation of students in the work of these organizations, as well as the benefits to be derived from forum discussions and religious exercises sponsored by these groups, serves to provide intellectual stimulation and spiritual guidance to a fairly large proportion of individuals.

Attitude of students toward the availability of a religious leader on the campus for help in solving religious and moral problems. It is one of the basic assumptions of this study that the presence of a competent religious leader and counselor on the college campus is fundamentally desirable and necessary if the college is to meet the all-round needs of the students. It is not enough for the college administrators merely to employ persons for this purpose. The students themselves must recognize in them the possibilities for guidance in the fundamental issues of religious living and spiritual health.

Besides raising the question with students regarding campus resources available for help in solving personal problems, it was decided, as an additional check on the question of whether the colleges were making adequate provisions at this point, to raise the following questions: "Is there a religious leader on the campus from whom you may seek help in the solution of your moral and spiritual problems? If not, do you feel the need of such a person?" A "yes" or "no" answer was provided to be checked by the respondents.

One thousand thirty-eight students, 77 per cent of the total number included in the study, responded "yes" to the first of these questions, while 239 students, 18 per cent, responded "no." Five per cent failed to provide data. The immediate conclusion on this point, therefore, is that, regardless of whether or not the students make adequate use of the counsel of the religious leader, the majority do recognize the availability of such a person on the campus. In answering this question, many students probably did not have in mind merely a director of religious life but any person on the college staff whom they considered capable of giving this kind of counsel.

Of the 239 students who answered "no" to the question of whether there was a religious leader on their campus from whom they could seek help in the solution of their moral and religious problems, 171, or 72 per cent, said "yes" to the question of whether they felt the need for such a person. Sixty-two, or 26 per cent, said that they did not feel the need for a religious leader. Two or three of these students indicated in their response that the religious leader they had on their campus was ineffective. At least two others said that they could not trust the appointed person with their difficulties.

It is significant that the largest percentage of students answering that they felt the need of a religious leader on their campus was in the public colleges, where also the largest proportion of students said that there was no such person on their campus. Seventy-seven per cent of the students of this group in the public colleges affirmed that they felt the need for a religious leader, as compared with 67 per cent in the church-related colleges and 53 per cent in the private institutions.

These figures and the comments given by students confirm the conclusions previously given; that is, the average student of this study, if not the average student in all colleges for Negroes, is fundamentally interested in religious values, and because of this fact the college has an inescapable obligation upon it to provide the most adequate resources in personnel and facilities for meeting the religious and moral needs of its constituency.

Courses students have found most helpful to their religious faith. Nearly three fourths of the students responded to the request, "List in the order of their significance the courses which you have found to be most helpful to your religious faith." The limitations involved in tabulating the returns made it necessary to record only the first course listed by the student, which from the point of view of the study is the most important.

Next to the courses in religion which, as may be expected, constituted those listed most frequently were courses in history, listed by 12 per cent of the respondents as seen in Table XX. It is apparent here that the study of history in some way, as far as the students of this study are concerned, carries with it the validation of religion as well as the clarification of its function in the historical process.

There is little correlation between the number of students majoring in the courses listed as being most helpful and the number of times these courses were listed. For example, the largest number of students responding to the questionnaire were majoring in education, yet this subject ranks eighth in the list of courses helpful to religious faith. The field of history comes closest to showing any correlation at this point. One hundred fifty-two students were majoring in this field, while 161 mentioned it as being most helpful to their religious faith. One would not deny, how-

TABLE XX

COURSES STUDENTS HAVE FOUND MOST HELPFUL TO THEIR
RELIGIOUS FAITH

Name of Course	Number of Times Mentioned
1. None	104
2. Religious courses	325
3. History	161
4. Philosophy	95
5. Sociology	94
6. Science courses	52
7. Psychology	47
8. English	34
9. Education	27
10. Music	8
11. Modern language	4
12. Home economics	4
13. Others	20
14. No answer	370
Total	1,345

ever, that the field of major specialization would be one of the determining factors as some students evaluate the courses most helpful to their
religious faith. For example, the largest percentage of students mention-
ing music were majors in this subject. Moreover, the personality and religious sympathy of the particular teacher will be one of the most important factors in any case. But the figures show that courses in religion,
history, philosophy, and sociology rank as most helpful to the religious
faith of students according to their own estimation.

*Members of the staff who most effectively influence the religious and
moral life of the students.* It is useful to discover not only what courses
students find most helpful to their religious faith but also what are the
academic interests or college responsibilities of the faculty and staff members who most effectively influence the religious and moral life of the
students. Students were asked, "Please list in the order of their significance the teachers or staff members who have most effectively influenced
your religious and moral life. (If you do not care to give the names of such
persons, give the field of their major work, for example, 'History teacher,'
'Bible teacher,' 'the coach.')"

The most influential teachers mentioned by the students correspond
roughly to the most helpful courses mentioned by them. That is to say,
the teachers in the fields of religion, history, sociology, and philosophy
stand out as the most helpful staff members religiously, just as the courses
taught by them stand out as being most helpful. The one exception, how-

ever, is in the case of teachers of education. While courses in education ranked eighth in the list of those most helpful to the religious life of students, the teachers of education ranked fourth among the most influential persons on the staff as far as the religious and moral life of the students was concerned.

Included among the persons mentioned a fairly large number of times were the college presidents themselves. These ranked third in the tabulation. Six per cent of the students said that the president was the most helpful staff member in the area of religion and morals. In some instances the president was mentioned a number of times by the students while in others he was not mentioned at all. Yet the fact that the name of the president ranks third on this list is quite significant. It suggests that, although he does not meet the students often, if at all, in the classroom, nevertheless, through chapel talks, or even by the general impression he makes upon them, as well as through personal contacts, he is able to inspire a fairly large number of students. It is also to be borne in mind that, out of 44 colleges from which information was available, 41 per cent of the presidents were licensed or ordained ministers. Three of these were in tax-supported schools.

The findings of this study indicate that the religious and moral influence exerted upon students by staff members is generally effected not primarily by virtue of common academic interests but rather by certain spiritual and moral qualities teachers possess and through which they inspire students toward higher ideals. Whether the teacher is professionally religious or has his major academic interests in science or languages or in any other field, he will, more often than he is aware, be a vital and determining factor in the shaping of the character of the students with whom he is associated.

Areas of thought in which changes in students' thinking have occurred. The college experience affects the thinking of the students at many points. In many instances by the time the student reaches the upper division of the college course his attitudes toward fundamental issues have been completely transformed.

In the study edited by Hartshorne, *From School to College,*[7] data were gathered from several hundred college youth in various institutions regarding the changes in their thinking on some of the crucial aspects of life and society. The table used in this study was appropriated, with one modification, for the purposes of the present investigation. In addition to the twelve "areas or subjects of thought" listed by the investigator in the Yale study of the transition experience, an area of thought termed "my attitude toward white people" was included in the present study in

---

7. Hugh Hartshorne, ed., *From School to College* (New Haven, Yale University Press, 1939).

order to determine to what extent, if any, Negro students are changing their attitudes with regard to this important area of adjustment. The statements calling for information on these points were as follows: "In their college experience many students find their thinking changing with reference to various aspects of life. Listed below are some of the areas in which such change often occurs. Please indicate by checking in the appropriate space the extent of such change in your own thinking."

The statistics of Table XXI show that there are four areas or subjects of thought with respect to which the thinking of at least 50 per cent of the students of this study has undergone "much change." In the order of their rank, these areas are "what life means to me, philosophy of life," the "value of college education for life," "science and man's place in the universe," and "the economic situation." It is natural that the thinking of students should be modified in the above areas, for they have very few definite concepts in regard to these aspects of thought at the beginning of their college career. The courses in science, the acquaintance with a new type of education, the increased sense of the social relations of humanity, as well as the enlarging historical perspective, all these inevitably result in the enlargement of the student's mind. He tends to see life as a whole. His world view takes on new meaning and his relationship to

TABLE XXI

AREAS OF THOUGHT IN WHICH CHANGES IN 1,345 STUDENTS' THINKING HAVE OCCURRED, ARRANGED ACCORDING TO RELATIVE EXTENT OF CHANGE

Area or Subject of Thought	Much Change	Little Change	No Change	No Answer
1. What life means to me: philosophy of life	755	357	108	125
2. Value of college education for life	720	326	182	117
3. Science and man's place in the universe	717	348	146	134
4. The economic situation	652	383	171	139
5. My life's work: vocation	554	363	260	168
6. Politics	520	372	286	167
7. Personal moral problems	438	545	217	145
8. Religion and its place in the social order	428	510	273	134
9. Relationships with the opposite sex	402	545	273	125
10. Marriage	392	401	401	151
11. Religion in your own life	348	532	355	110
12. Prayer	343	394	465	143
13. My attitude toward white people	340	425	473	95

society tends to become more clearly defined. This is as it should be in college education.

Among the least-affected areas of thought was that of prayer. It appears that the average student of this study was only slightly affected in his thought about religion in general. It would seem, in view of the admitted change with respect to "science and man's place in the universe," that a corresponding change would occur in the student's ideas of prayer. Since this is not the case, it is apparent that students' attitudes toward religion vary relatively little between their freshman and senior years. That some modification at this point occurs is evident, as already shown in the discussion of outstanding religious and ethical problems faced by students. Among the largest percentage of religious problems and difficult experiences for this group were those in the area of readjustment to new theological concepts. Yet it is clear that the modifications are not serious enough in the students' minds to be designated by the expression "much change."

The findings of the present investigation are strikingly similar to those in the Yale study of the transition experience, with respect to both the areas in which the largest number of students indicated much change in their thinking and those areas of thought in which little change had occurred. Upon analyzing the returns from sophomore students, the writers of the transition study report found that:

The most radical changes in more than half the students, occurred in thought about what life means and the economic situation. Politics came next, then science, the relations with the opposite sex, then personal moral problems, and then religion in its social aspects. Thought about religion as a personal affair and about prayer changed least of all.[8]

One of the significant results of this part of the study is the discovery that the area in which students indicated that the least amount of change had occurred was that of "my attitude toward white people"; only 25 per cent of the respondents checked the space "much change." On the other hand, 32 per cent checked "little change" while 35 per cent indicated that no change had taken place in their thinking with regard to their attitudes toward the dominant group. Negro college students' average contacts with members of the dominant group do not generally serve to modify their attitudes toward them. Some students, however, develop new points of view through certain interracial experiences which they may have in intercollegiate conferences. It is doubtless true that for both Negro and white students the greatest modification of racial attitudes occurs through participation in interracial student gatherings. Since most of

8. *Ibid.*, p. 273.

such gatherings are sponsored by some national, regional, or local religious organization, the modification of racial attitudes may be attributed to religious forces. Certainly for the youth of college age creative work is needed in the area of racial attitudes. It will admittedly be relatively difficult to change attitudes that are born and nurtured in an unfavorable social setting. There are thousands of Negro youth who have had no pleasant contact or experience with a white person. It is, therefore, a revelation to them to have the opportunity of meeting members of the dominant group who show toward them a spirit of Christian understanding and brotherhood. Such opportunities should be provided for Negro youth. It will be the means for helping to do away with some of the prejudices and bitterness which are inevitably a part of the psychological make-up of large numbers of Negro Americans. The college that does its job well in this area will seek to inspire Negro youth toward an understanding of the difficulties in the area of race relations and will seek to equip him with the knowledge and the technique by means of which racial prejudices may be alleviated; and, at the same time, it will seek to give him a spiritual dynamic adequate for maintaining his equilibrium in the midst of a hostile society.

The final item on the student questionnaire was a request that students indicate, in the order of their significance, the areas where the most important changes in their thinking had occurred. There is a strong correlation between these areas and the extent of the changes of thought in various fields. For example, the areas in which the students indicated that the greatest changes had occurred were those of "what life means to me," "science and man's place in the universe," "personal moral problems," and "my life's work."

It is significant to note that the area where the smallest number of students indicated that the most important changes had occurred was that of "my attitude toward white people." Only twenty-four students said that the most important changes for them had occurred in this area.

In general, it may be said that the students of this study indicate change of thought along some of the fundamental areas of life, showing that the college is affecting their attitudes at quite important points. The majority have undergone changes in at least four significant areas and among the fewest number of changes were those in the area of religion. The writers of the Yale transition study report came to conclusions similar to those found here, especially in the case of changes in religious thought. They asserted that "Taking all the facts reported into consideration, of all the things that happen to students in college, religious thought seems to be little subject to change, at least during the freshman year, although shifts are occurring in valuations which an observer would probably regard as religious. That is, religion, as understood by college men, seems to be a rather static affair. . . ." [9]

The findings of the present chapter are also in line with conclusions reached by Rollo May in his study at Michigan State College. Among other things, May drew the following generalizations: "It is an error to assert that students as a whole tend to be irreligious. The great majority believe in God and nine out of ten believe in the value of religion for society and for their personal lives. The students we believe represent more genuine religion than any cross section of the adult non-college population of the country." [10]

In line with studies made by Artman, Edwards, and Fisher, and also the Katz and Allport study, May decides that "college does not make atheists." A third conclusion to which May's study led was: "The college experience is not responsible for as great a dropping off in church attendance on the part of students as is generally assumed. Almost half of the men students on this campus are to be found in church on Sunday morning." [11]

9. R. R. May, "Portrait of Men Students," *Christian Education*, XIX (April, June, 1936), 399.

10. *Ibid.*, p. 402.

11. *Ibid.*

X

FINDINGS AND RECOMMENDATIONS

STARTING out largely after the Civil War as expressions of the missionary spirit, the Negro colleges have made progress commensurate with the general social and economic development of the racial group as a whole. The rise of these institutions parallels the pattern of that in other colleges. In each case the emphasis was put primarily on the training of ministers and, later, on the training of a religiously educated laity. The development of tax-supported institutions for Negroes, although begun relatively late, has nevertheless been fairly rapid in proportion to the simultaneous growth of church-related and private colleges. Today it is estimated that there are around 40,000 youth enrolled in 108 colleges for Negroes. The public colleges, comprising only 34 per cent of the total, enroll more than 50 per cent of the collegiate population. The consideration of the religious attitudes and provisions in the best accredited higher institutions for Negroes has resulted in the following findings.

1. Because of the caste society in which Negroes live, there are fundamental psychological, social, and spiritual problems which the youth of this minority face. The religious program of the college has an indispensable role to play in the solution of the problems of personality adjustment which are engendered by a caste society.

2. The statements of the objectives of Negro colleges include, for the most part, the same general emphases which other colleges claim. On the part of only a small number of institutions is there any declared recognition in the statement of objectives of the peculiar problems incident to the racial background of their constituents. There is indication, however, of increasing emphases being made at this point. More and more leaders in Negro higher education are pointing out the peculiar role of the Negro college in preparing its students for leadership in widening the advantages inherent in a democratic society. Fewer colleges are making specific references to religious objectives than was the case formerly. Yet it is probable that some of those colleges which did not include any reference to religion in their statements of objectives put more emphasis upon it than their failure to mention religion implies.

3. According to their claims, Negro college administrators in all types of institutions are as a whole committed to the principle that religion is an indispensable part of education. Presidents of some state colleges, where legal restrictions against inclusion of religion in their programs

are felt, make a special effort, nevertheless, to provide opportunities for religious training through compulsory and voluntary religious chapel as well as Sunday-school exercises. This is a demonstration of the conviction that religion in some way must be recognized as a part of the total program of the college. Yet, for various reasons, the declared interest by certain college administrators in the essential place of religion in education is not always matched by effective provisions for it. It was observed during this study that, in spite of an insistence by certain college administrators that religion is fundamental in education, few provisions in the area of personnel workers or religious chapel programs were made for the development of religious attitudes. It is recognized that for the state institutions particularly the inclusion of religious programs involves extra effort in the raising of funds to carry on this work.

4. Discussions with faculty members individually and in groups revealed that they were generally agreed that the place of religious training is fundamental in the program of the college. These discussions point to the conclusion that by and large there is an interest in religion exhibited by faculty members. But there is without doubt in many instances a failure to give concrete expression to a declared interest in religion. This is corroborated in the estimate of the religious insincerity of the faculty which students made in a later part of the study. Among certain teachers in these schools there does exist a spirit of indifference to religion which is no doubt due in part to unacquaintance with this aspect of man's experience. The outspoken critics of religion, however, are relatively few.

5. In practically all the colleges of this study some types of administrative provisions for religion are to be found. These include chapel programs, Sunday-school exercises, prayer meetings, weeks of prayer, religious directors, and courses in religion. Even in some state institutions compulsory religious exercises are sponsored. Moreover, a number of institutions are following the practice of having faculty and students coöperate in planning the religious exercises of the college. Yet only a small number reported a well-ordered system of personal counseling for students. Seventy-five per cent of the colleges of this study employed some such worker as a director of religious life or chaplain. In most cases these officers had teaching responsibilities in religion or in related fields. In a number of institutions from two to five other instructors devoted all or part of their time to teaching courses in religion. In scholastic preparation as well as in academic rating the teachers of religion ranked relatively high as compared with teachers in other fields. Although they did not rank as high as teachers in the colleges for the nation as a whole, they did compare favorably with other teachers in the colleges of this study.

Around 64 per cent of the institutions surveyed provide courses in religion for college studies. Three additional institutions offer non-credit courses in this field. Thirty-four per cent of the colleges require courses in religion for graduation while 33 per cent offer enough for a major in religion. Courses in some aspect of Biblical study rank first both in regard to the total number of courses offered and total number of students enrolled. These courses also rank first with respect to the types of courses for which requirements for graduation are made. Only three tax-supported colleges of this study offered any credit courses in religion.

6. In all but one of the schools of this study voluntary religious organizations for the students are to be found. Most of these are affiliated with either the Y.M.C.A. or Y.W.C.A. The total number of all voluntary organizations averages approximately three per college. The average membership in voluntary organizations is estimated nominally as around 49 students for each group. The organizations sponsor mainly such activities as religious services, forums, study groups, social service programs, and informal entertainments.

The participation of Negro students in interracial conferences was indicated in a number of institutions. It is felt that this is one of the most important ways in which the mutual understanding requisite for transcending many of the difficulties of caste may be fostered.

7. Thirty-one institutions reported an average appropriation for religious work of $3,266.08. Proportionately the private colleges, followed by the church-related institutions, budgeted more for religious work than did the publicly supported colleges. The largest item was for teachers' salaries. Yet the salary scale in the institutions of this survey was, in general, relatively low when compared with figures for the nation as a whole. The average budget for the fifty student organizations making reports was $182.77 each. This amount, obviously, is hardly adequate to enable each organization effectively to carry on an all-round religious program. The range of budgets was from $25 to $900 for each organization. The statistics for the budgetary provisions by both the college administrations and student organizations reflect the financial limitations that are characteristic of Negro education in general.

8. The study of 1,345 students in 33 colleges revealed that a large percentage were church members and attended church fairly regularly when at home, participating in various types of activities. As many as 44 per cent of them belonged to the Baptist denomination and an additional 30 per cent were members of some branch of the Methodist Church. Only a small percentage were Catholics or without any church affiliation at all. The students who have had courses in religion were generally appreciative of them. Many more were willing to describe them as "interesting" or "fascinating" than as "unstimulating" or "dull." This fact attests to an interest in the content of religious courses as much as it does to the

quality of teaching in these courses. Yet students tend to describe the attitude of their fellow students toward religion as "indifferent"; but the findings of other parts of this investigation refute this estimate.

9. Eighty per cent of the undergraduates were able to list one or more benefits to be derived from the chapel program. These benefits were chiefly those in the areas of worship and the development of the devotional life, instruction in religion and culture, and broadening contacts with outstanding leaders. It is significant that they were much less able to give pointed criticisms of chapel than they were to state benefits in it. The major criticisms given were that the exercises were monotonous, poorly planned with no appeal to student interests and needs, and that they were compulsory. There were a few students who expressed the criticism that the chapel exercises were too often lacking in the religious element. As many as 64 per cent of the undergraduates of this study claimed that they would attend chapel services regularly if the services were put on a voluntary basis.

10. Forty-six per cent of the students of this study expressed the view that the college administration and staff did not exemplify a genuine religious spirit in the carrying on of their activities and responsibilities. The smallest number, 35 per cent, expressing this view were in the church-related institutions while the largest number, 52 per cent, were in the public colleges.

11. The religious and ethical problems which students said they faced in their college life, as well as the experiences which they enumerated as being hindrances to the development of their religious faith, were most often those which can be classified as in the realm of religious thought. Students were able to list a number of resources in the college which were available for help in the solution of their personal problems. The majority of these were faculty counselors, the deans of men, the religious directors, and the voluntary religious organizations. The courses listed by them as being most helpful to the development of their religious faith were largely those in religion, history, philosophy, sociology, and the sciences. The members of the staff whom the students listed as being most helpful to the development of their religious life were primarily the religious workers, followed by teachers in the field of history, the college president, teachers of education, sociology, English, and philosophy, and the deans of men. The students of this study demonstrate that the college has influenced their thinking in various areas, chief among which are the areas of science and man's place in the universe, what life means to them, and value of college education for life and the economic situation. Much change was indicated as taking place in these areas by at least 50 per cent of the 1,345 students. Fewest changes occurred in the areas of religion in their own lives, prayer, and attitudes toward white people.

12. Among both teachers and administrators there was a general conclusion that Negro college students have a deep-seated yearning for the fruits of religion. In spite of the fact that students do not have much to say publicly about this yearning, it was the general conclusion that underneath much of the pretended indifference was a deep-seated interest. In general the results of the survey of the attitudes of the students toward the religious life of the campus corroborate this view. A review of all the problems and hindering experiences mentioned supports the opinion that there is an interest in religion on the part of college students which is not apparent on the surface. At the same time, the findings suggest that the colleges are not providing as many adequate opportunities for religious development as appear desirable in view of the total social setting and ultimate objectives of higher education among Negroes.

RECOMMENDATIONS

THE total religious program in any college should be conceived not in terms merely of the formal presentation of religion in courses or in chapel exercises or even in the encouragement of religious organizations. These may be evidences of a religious spirit but do not at all constitute the total means by which the college will attempt to exemplify and to inculcate religious ideals. To be profoundly religious it is encumbent upon the institution to see to it that religion functions throughout its total programs and services, its relationships not only with the students and faculty but with employees and with all those forces in the community which the college may touch in any way. It has been well stated by one observer that in the matter of housing of students, the food which is served in the dining room, the remuneration for work opportunities offered to students, the athletic program and other extracurricular activities, as well as in sincere attempts to provide the most satisfying educational program, the college should at all points attempt to carry out the religious spirit. In other words, attempts should be made not to compartmentalize the concept or the practice of religion but to inculcate the highest spiritual ideals in the totality of the experiences by and through which the college influences its constituents. In this sense the entire budget of the university will be devoted to essentially religious ideals.

1. The college for Negroes, if it is to be effective, must take account of the various environmental factors which help to condition the life of the student before, during, as well as after his college experience. This means, among other things, that the college administrators will be interested not only in the mechanics of the college program but, above all, in the personality growth and adjustment of each student. This principle is in keeping with the Christian doctrine of the inherent worth of personality.

The objectives of the college should be conceived, stated, and pursued in the light of this fundamental principle. In the matter of the selection of teachers as well as of students, college authorities will be guided by their devotion to these essentially religious ideals and aims. The college has the task of providing a total curriculum which will help the student to attain a world view as well as those spiritual bases for personal growth necessary for participating most effectively in his environment of a class and caste society. Unless this is done in all colleges for Negroes, without respect to type of control, one of the most fundamental opportunities for creative education will be lost.

2. It is apparent from the students' own estimates of the religious sincerity of college authorities and teachers that to a great extent the latter have failed to convince students of their honesty and integrity. Obviously the college authorities need to examine this criticism with humility and to make whatever modifications each particular situation requires in order to insure that, through the course provisions of the college, as well as in the relationships between faculty and students, and among faculty members themselves, undergraduates will become conscious of the ideals of religion sincerely determining the attitudes and policies of the campus community.

3. The need of adequate financial resources for the improvement of the presentation of religion in Negro colleges is apparent along at least five different lines. These are (1) the need for development and support of a trained faculty leadership for religious work among students; (2) the need for providing resources for developing adequate campus programs among students which will serve to provide opportunities for religious expression and creative personality adjustments; (3) the need for stimulating and developing student morale through such means as conferences for the study of some of the living issues which affect students; (4) the need for scholarships for students interested in giving themselves to the service of religion; and (5) the development of departments of religion in the colleges and universities.

The need for developing and supporting trained faculty leadership for religious work among students is of strategic importance at the present time. Within relatively recent years the colleges have been busily engaged in trying to meet the rigorous standards of the various accrediting agencies and this has led to increased emphasis upon the so-called secular subjects and decreasing emphasis upon or the neglect of courses and programs having to do with religion. This is particularly unfortunate in those schools which are supposed to be under the influence and support of the forces of religion. Many colleges have no well-planned religious program for students. The religious life of the campus is often left to some member of the staff who already is overburdened with a heavy teaching schedule and who frequently has no specialized training for this important work.

4. In view of the unmistakably latent concern for religious values on the part of students the college should spare no pains to work out effective means for the development of wholesome, creative avenues of religious expression and for giving this interest in things spiritual adequate direction. Faculty-student coöperation in planning the religious life of the campus should be fostered. The college should employ and invite to the campus the best available religious leaders who can guide the students' spiritual growth and inspire them toward increasing spiritual achievements. Increasing emphasis should be placed upon the development of adequate, systematic counseling provisions for students, which the students themselves will recognize as among the most important aspects of the resources of the college. More encouragement and assistance need to be given student religious organizations through the appointment of competent faculty advisers and through help in the working out of adequate budgets for effective religious activities. The college owes it to the students to help them work out a voluntary program that will embody the kind of spiritual dynamic and call forth the spirit of heroic and sacrificial leadership demanded by the present social status of Negro youth. Especially is this true in the state schools, since Negro denominations are hardly prepared to take an active part in establishing religious work in these colleges.

5. It is also recommended that colleges not only be concerned with financing religious provisions for students but at the same time should provide opportunities for developing the religious life of faculty members themselves.

6. The continuing interest in and planning for the effective presentation of religion on the campus will be enhanced by the getting together of faculty members who have responsibilities in this area. Some such organization as the Fellowship of Religious Workers in Colleges for Negroes, begun a few years ago, should be of inestimable value in developing more effective ways and means for making the religious life of the colleges increasingly effective.

APPENDIX

A. COLLEGES INCLUDED IN CATALOGUE STUDY
OF OBJECTIVES

CHURCH-RELATED

Bennett College, Greensboro, North Carolina
Bishop College, Marshall, Texas
Johnson C. Smith University, Charlotte, North Carolina
Knoxville College, Knoxville, Tennessee
Lane College, Jackson, Tennessee
Livingstone College, Salisbury, North Carolina
Morehouse College, Atlanta, Georgia
Philander Smith College, Little Rock, Arkansas
Samuel Huston College, Austin, Texas
Shaw University, Raleigh, North Carolina
St. Augustine College, Raleigh, North Carolina
Talladega College, Talladega, Alabama
Tillotson College, Austin, Texas
Tougaloo College, Tougaloo, Mississippi
Virginia Union University, Richmond, Virginia
Wilberforce University, Wilberforce University, Ohio
Wiley College, Marshall, Texas
Xavier University, New Orleans, Louisiana

PRIVATE

Dillard University, New Orleans, Louisiana
Fisk University, Nashville, Tennessee
Florida Normal and Industrial Institute, St. Augustine, Florida
Hampton Institute, Hampton, Virginia
Lincoln University, Lincoln University, Pennsylvania
Spelman College, Atlanta, Georgia
Tuskegee Institute, Tuskegee, Alabama

PUBLIC

Agricultural and Technical College, Greensboro, North Carolina
Agricultural, Mechanical and Normal College, Pine Bluff, Arkansas
Florida Agricultural and Mechanical College, Tallahassee, Florida
Howard University, Washington, D.C.
Kentucky State College, Frankfort, Kentucky
Lincoln University, Jefferson City, Missouri

Louisville Municipal College, Louisville, Kentucky
Miner Teachers College, Washington, D.C.
Morgan State College, Baltimore, Maryland
North Carolina State College for Negroes, Durham, North Carolina
Prairie View Normal and Industrial College, Prairie View, Texas
Southern University, Scotlandville, Louisiana
State Agricultural and Mechanical College, Orangeburg, South Carolina
State Agricultural and Mechanical College, Normal, Alabama
State College for Colored Students, Dover, Delaware
Tennessee Agricultural and Industrial College, Nashville, Tennessee
Virginia State College for Negroes, Ettrick, Virginia

B. COLLEGES SUPPLYING COMPLETE OR PARTIAL DATA ON ADMINISTRATIVE PROVISIONS FOR RELIGION AND VOLUNTARY STUDENT RELIGIOUS ORGANIZATIONS [1]

I. Church-Related

Class A

Bennett College
Johnson C. Smith University
Le Moyne College
Morehouse College
Talladega College
Virginia Union University
Wilberforce University
Wiley College

Others

Bishop College
Clark College
Knoxville College
Lane College
Leland College
Livingstone College
Morris Brown College
Paine College
Shaw University
St. Augustine College
Texas College
Tillotson College

II. Private

Class A

Dillard University
Fisk University
Hampton Institute
Lincoln University (Pa.)
Tuskegee Institute

III. Public

Class A

Agricultural and Technical College, Greensboro, N.C.
Florida Agricultural and Mechanical College
Harriet B. Stowe College
Howard University
Kentucky State College
Lincoln University (Mo.)
Louisville Municipal College
Morgan State College
North Carolina State College for Negroes
Prairie View Normal and Industrial College
Southern University

1. The rating of these schools is given as of the school year 1940–41.

Virginia State College

West Virginia State College

Others

Alabama State College

Alcorn Agricultural and Mechanical College

Bowie State Teachers College

Colored Agricultural and Normal University

Elizabeth City State Teachers College

South Carolina State College

C. SIXTEEN CLASS A COLLEGES SELECTED FOR PERSONAL VISITATION

Church-related Location	Present or Historical Religious Affiliation	Enrollment '40–'41
1. Bennett College, Greensboro, N.C.	Meth. Epis.	303
2. Johnson C. Smith University, Charlotte, N.C.	Pres., U.S.A.	400
3. Morehouse College, Atlanta, Ga.	No. Baptist [1]	415
4. Talladega College, Talladega, Ala.	Cong. Chr.	269
5. Virginia Union University, Richmond, Va.	No. Baptist	607
6. Wilberforce University, Wilberforce, O.	A.M.E. [2]	664
Private		N
1. Fisk University, Nashville, Tenn.	Cong. Chr.	380
2. Hampton Institute, Hampton, Va.	Cong. Chr.	899
3. Tuskegee Institute, Tuskegee, Ala.		1,392
4. Lincoln University, Chester Co., Pa.	Pres. U.S.A.	389
Public		
1. Agricultural and Technical College, Greensboro, N.C.	Cong. Chr.	950
2. Kentucky State College, Frankfort, Ky.		519
3. Morgan State College, Baltimore, Md.	Meth. Epis.	428
4. Virginia State College, Petersburg, Va.		1,072
5. West Virginia State College, Institute, W. Va.		943
6. Howard University, Washington, D.C.	Cong. Chr. [3]	2,600
	Total Enrollment	12,230

1. Although control of Morehouse College was relinquished to the Board of Trustees in 1935, it was considered in this study and listed here as a church-related college because of the strong Baptist tradition which has long been and still is associated with the school. Members of the original controlling body, the American Baptist Home Mission Society, are represented on the Board of Trustees.

2. While Wilberforce is predominantly under the control of the African Methodist Episcopal Church, support for part of its work is appropriated by the State of Ohio.

3. Technically, Howard University is under the private control of its Board of Trustees but, in view of the fact that its background has long been associated primarily with the Federal Government and that more than half of its support comes from public funds, it was considered, for the purposes of this study, as a public institution.

D. THIRTY-THREE COLLEGES IN WHICH 1,345 STUDENTS FILLED OUT QUESTIONNAIRES ON THE RELIGIOUS LIFE OF THE CAMPUS

I. CHURCH-RELATED

1. Benedict College
2. Bennett College
3. Bishop College
4. Johnson C. Smith University
5. Livingstone College
6. Morehouse College
7. Morris College
8. Morris Brown College
9. Shaw University
10. Talladega College
11. Tillotson College
12. Virginia Union University
13. Wilberforce University

II. PRIVATE

1. Fisk University
2. Hampton Institute
3. Lincoln University (Pa.)
4. Spelman College
5. Tuskegee Institute

III. PUBLIC

1. Agricultural and Technical College, Greensboro, N.C.
2. Alcorn College
3. Bowie State Teachers College
4. Elizabeth City State Teachers College
5. Fayetteville State Teachers College
6. Florida Agricultural and Mechanical College
7. Howard University
8. Kentucky State College
9. Lincoln University (Mo.)
10. Morgan State College
11. Prairie View Normal and Industrial College
12. Southern University
13. Tennessee Agricultural and Industrial College
14. Virginia State College
15. West Virginia State College

E. LIST OF COLLEGES CONTRIBUTING TO THE
PUBLICATION OF THIS STUDY

Agricultural and Mechanical College	Pine Bluff, Ark.
Agricultural and Technical College	Greensboro, N.C.
Alcorn College	Alcorn, Miss.
Barber Scotia College	Concord, N.C.
Bishop College	Marshall, Texas
Claflin College	Orangeburg, S.C.
Dillard University	New Orleans, La.
Fisk University	Nashville, Tenn.
Florida Normal College	St. Augustine, Fla.
Georgia Normal	Albany, Georgia
Hampton Institute	Hampton, Virginia
Howard University	Washington, D.C.
Kentucky State College	Frankfort, Ky.
Knoxville College	Knoxville, Tenn.
Langston University	Langston, Okla.
Le Moyne College	Memphis, Tenn.
Lincoln University	Lincoln, Pa.
Livingstone College	Salisbury, N.C.
Miles Memorial College	Birmingham, Ala.
Morehouse College	Atlanta, Georgia
Morris College	Sumter, S.C.
Paine College	Augusta, Georgia
Philander Smith College	Little Rock, Ark.
Saint Augustine College	Raleigh, N.C.
Saint Paul's Polytechnic Inst.	Lawrenceville, Va.
State Normal College	Normal, Ala.
Storer College	Harpers Ferry, W.Va.
Tennessee State College	Nashville, Tennessee
Virginia State College	Petersburg, Va.
Virginia Union University	Richmond, Va.

BIBLIOGRAPHY

A. BOOKS AND PAMPHLETS

ANGELL, ROBERT C., *The Campus*. New York, D. Appleton & Co., 1928. 239 pp.

A Statement of Facts Respecting the School for Colored Females in Canterbury, Connecticut, together with a Report of the Late Trial of Miss Prudence Crandall. Brooklyn, Connecticut, Advertiser Press, 1833. Pamphlet.

ATWOOD, J. W., *et al.*, *Thus Be Their Destiny*. Washington, American Council on Education, 1941. 96 pp.

BEDE, BROTHER, *A Study of the Development of Negro Education under Catholic Auspices in Maryland and the District of Columbia*. Baltimore, Johns Hopkins University Press, 1935. 125 pp.

BETTS, C. H., *Teaching Religion Today*. New York, Abingdon Press, 1934. 268 pp.

BIXLER, JULIUS SEELYE, *Can Religion Be Taught?* The National Council on Religion in Higher Education, Bulletin IX. New York, 1935. Pamphlet.

BLOSE, DAVID, and CALIVER, AMBROSE, *Statistics of the Education of Negroes*, United States Office of Education Bulletin, 1938, No. 13. Washington, United States Government Printing Office, 1939.

BOND, C. H., *A Study of the Religious Attitudes of 500 College Students*. New York, Bucknell University and the Board of Education of the Northern Baptist Convention, 1939. Pamphlet.

———— *The Liberal Arts College Functioning in the Field of Religion*. The National Council on Religion in Higher Education, Bulletin X. New York, 1935. Pamphlet.

BOND, HORACE MANN, *The Education of the Negro in the American Social Order*. New York, Prentice-Hall Co., 1934. 501 pp.

BOWER, W. C., *The Curriculum of Religious Education*. New York, Charles Scribner's Sons, 1925. 283 pp.

BOYER, EDWARD S., *Religion in the American College*. New York, Abingdon Press, 1930. 105 pp.

BRAWLEY, B. G., *A Social History of the American Negro*. New York, Macmillan Co., 1921. 311 pp.

BROWN, S. W., *The Secularization of American Education*. New York, Teachers College, Columbia University, 1912. 160 pp.

BRUBACHER, JOHN S., *Modern Philosophies of Education*. New York, McGraw-Hill Co., 1939. 370 pp.

CALIVER, AMBROSE, *A Background Study of Negro College Students.* United States Office of Education Bulletin, 1933, No. 8. Washington, United States Government Printing Office, 1933. 117 pp.

—— *A Personnel Study of Negro College Students.* New York, Bureau of Publications, Teachers College, Columbia University, 1931. 146 pp.

CASWELL, H. L., and CAMPBELL, D. S., *Curriculum Development.* New York, American Book Co., 1935. 600 pp.

CHARTERS, W. W., *The Teaching of Ideals.* New York, Macmillan Co., 1927. 372 pp.

CLARK, FELTON C., *The Control of State-Supported Teacher-Training Programs for Negroes.* New York, Bureau of Publications, Teachers College, Columbia University, 1934. 103 pp.

CLARK, GEORGE L., *A History of Connecticut.* New York, G. P. Putnam's Sons, 1914. 565 pp.

COE, G. A., *Educating for Citizenship.* New York, Charles Scribner's Sons, 1932. 205 pp.

COUNTS, G. S., *Dare the School Build a New Social Order?* New York, John Day Co., 1932. 56 pp.

—— *The Social Foundations of Education.* New York, Charles Scribner's Sons, 1934. 579 pp.

CUBBERLEY, E. P., *A Brief History of Education.* Boston, Houghton Mifflin Co., 1922. 455 pp.

—— *Public Education in the United States.* Revised ed. Boston, Riverside Press, 1934. 782 pp.

CURNOCK, NEHEMIAH, ed., *The Journal of the Rev. John Wesley, A.M.,* Vols. I and IV. London, Epworth Press, 1938. 8 vols.

DANIEL, W. A., *The Education of Negro Ministers.* New York, George H. Doran Co., 1925. 187 pp.

DAVIS, ALLISON, and DOLLARD, JOHN, *Children of Bondage: The Personality Development of Negro Youth in the Urban South.* Washington, American Council on Education, 1940. 294 pp.

DIGGS, M. A., *Catholic Negro Education in the United States.* Washington, published by the author, 1936. 185 pp.

DOLLARD, JOHN, *Caste and Class in a Southern Town.* New Haven, Yale University Press, 1937. 498 pp.

DU BOIS, W. E. B., *The College Bred Negro American.* Atlanta, Atlanta University Press, 1910. 104 pp.

Education Adequate for Modern Times. Discussions and Proposals of National Student Faculty Conference, Detroit, 1930. New York, Association Press, 1931. 276 pp.

Educational Directory, United States Office of Education Bulletin, 1940, No. 1, Part III. Washington, United States Government Printing Office, 1940, 85 pp.

Educational Policies Commission, *The Unique Function of Education in American Democracy*. Washington, The Educational Policies Commission, 1937. 129 pp.

EDWARDS, RICHARD HENRY, *Three Basic Realizations about Religion at State Universities*. Ithaca, Cornell Coöperative Society, 1940. Pamphlet.

———— and HILGARD, E. R., *Student Counseling*. The National Council on Religion in Higher Education, Bulletin VII. Ithaca, 1928. 64 pp.

———— ARTMAN, J. M., FISHER, GALEN M., *Undergraduates*. New York, Doubleday, Doran & Co., 1928. 368 pp.

FARR, MAUDE, *College Salaries, 1939–40*. Federal Security Agency, United States Office of Education, Circular No. 196. Washington, 1940. 33 pp.

FITZPATRICK, E. A., ed., *Readings in the Philosophy of Education*. New York, D. Appleton-Century Co., 1936. 809 pp.

FLEXNER, ABRAHAM, *Universities, American, English and German*. Oxford, Oxford University Press, 1930. 381 pp.

FOERSTER, NORMAN, *The American State University*. Chapel Hill, University of North Carolina Press, 1937. 287 pp.

FOREMAN, CLARK, *Environmental Factors in Negro Elementary Education*. New York, W. W. Norton & Co., 1932. 83 pp.

FRAZIER, E. F., *Negro Youth at the Crossways: Their Personality Development in the Middle States*. Washington, American Council on Education, 1940.

GALLAGHER, BUELL G., *American Caste and the Negro College*. New York, Columbia University Press, 1938. 444 pp.

HARRIS, CYRIL, *The Religion of Undergraduates*. New York, Charles Scribner's Sons, 1925. 57 pp.

HARTSHORNE, HUGH, ed., *From School to College*. New Haven, Yale University Press, 1939. 446 pp.

———— et al., *Standards and Trends in Religious Education*. New Haven, Yale University Press, 1933. 230 pp.

HITES, LAIRD T., *The Effective Christian College*. New York, Macmillan Co., 1925. 198 pp.

HOCKING, W. E., "Can Values Be Taught?" *Obligations of the Universities to the Social Order*. New York, New York University Press, 1933. 503 pp.

HOLMES, D. O. W., *The Evolution of the Negro College*. New York, Bureau of Publications, Teachers College, Columbia University, 1934. 221 pp.

HORNE, H. H., *The Democratic Philosophy of Education*. New York, Macmillan Co., 1932. 547 pp.

HUDELSON, EARL, ed., *Problems of College Education*. Minneapolis, University of Minnesota Press, 1928. 449 pp.

HUTCHINS, ROBERT M., *The Higher Learning in America*. New Haven, Yale University Press, 1936. 119 pp.

JACKS, M. L., *God in Education*. London, Rich & Cowan, 1939. 240 pp.

JACKSON, J. K., and MALMBERG, C. F., *Religious Education and the State*. Garden City, Doubleday, Doran & Co., 1928. 195 pp.

JOHNSON, C. S., *Growing Up in the Black Belt*. Washington, American Council on Education, 1941. 360 pp.

——— *The Negro in American Civilization*. New York, Henry Holt & Co., 1930. 538 pp.

——— *The Negro College Graduate*. Chapel Hill, University of North Carolina Press, 1938. 377 pp.

JOHNSTON, J. B., *The Liberal College in Changing Society*. New York, Century Co., 1930. 326 pp.

JONES, CHARLES C., *The Religious Instruction of Negroes in the United States*. Savannah, Thomas Purse, 1842. 277 pp.

JONES, T. J., *Negro Education, A Study of the Private and Higher Schools for Colored People in the United States*. United States Office of Education Bulletins, Nos. 38 and 39. Washington, United States Government Printing Office, 1916. 2 vols. 724 pp.

JUDD, CHARLES N., *Education and Social Progress*. New York, Harcourt, Brace & Co., 1934. 276 pp.

KATZ, DAVID, ALLPORT, F. H., and JENNESS, M. B., *Students' Attitudes*. Syracuse, Crofts Press, 1931. 408 pp.

KELLY, F. J., *The American Arts College*. New York, Macmillan Co., 1925. 198 pp.

KELLY, ROBERT L., ed., *The Effective College*. New York, Association of American Colleges, 1928. 302 pp.

KENT, C. F., *Undergraduate Courses in Religion at the Tax-Supported Colleges and Universities of America*. The National Council on Religion in Higher Education, Bulletin IV. New York, 1924. 34 pp.

——— *Religion at a Great State University*. The National Council on Religion in Higher Education, Bulletin III. New York, 1923. 11 pp.

KENT, Raymond A., ed., *Higher Education in America*. New York, Ginn & Co., 1930. 689 pp.

KILPATRICK, W. H., *Education for a Changing Civilization.* New York, Macmillan Co., 1927. 143 pp.

KLEIN, A. J., *Survey of Negro Colleges and Universities.* United States Bureau of Education Bulletin, 1926, No. 7. Washington, United States Government Printing Office, 1928. 964 pp.

KOTSCHNIG, WALTER M., *The University in a Changing World.* Oxford, Oxford University Press, 1932. 224 pp.

LEAVELL, U. W., *Philanthropy in Negro Education.* Nashville, George Peabody College for Teachers, 1930. 188 pp.

LITTLE, CLARENCE C., *The Awakening College.* New York, W. W. Norton & Co., 1930. 282 pp.

MARITAIN, JACQUES, *et al., Religion and the Modern World.* Philadelphia, University of Pennsylvania Press, 1941. 192 pp.

MAYS, B. E., and NICHOLSON, J. W., *The Negro's Church.* New York, Institute of Social and Religious Study and Research, 1933. 292 pp.

McCUISTON, FRED S., *Graduate Instruction for Negroes in the United States.* Nashville, George Peabody College for Teachers, 1939. 172 pp.

——— *Higher Education for Negroes.* Nashville, Committee on Approved Schools, 1933. 40 pp.

McKINNEY, T. E., ed., *Higher Education among Negroes.* Charlotte, Johnson C. Smith University, 1932. 124 pp.

MORGAN, W. H., *Student Religion during Fifty Years.* New York, Association Press, 1936. 233 pp.

NATHAN, M., *The Attitude of the Jewish Student Towards His Religion.* New York, Bloch Publishing Co., 1932. 264 pp.

New Direction. Report of the National Student Assembly, Oxford, Ohio, 1937. New York, Association Press, 1938.

PATTON, L. K., *The Purposes of Church-Related Colleges.* New York, Teachers College Contribution to Education, No. 783. Bureau of Publications, Teachers College, Columbia University, 1940. 287 pp.

Qualifications and Training for the Secretaryship of the Y.M.C.A. New York, Association Press, 1941. Pamphlet.

Racial Inequalities in Education. New York, National Association for the Advancement of Colored People, 1938. Pamphlet.

REEVES, FLOYD W., and RUSSELL, J. D., *College Organization and Administration.* Indianapolis, Board of Education, Disciples of Christ, 1929. 324 pp.

REID, IRA DEA., *In a Minor Key: Negro Youth in Story and Fact.* Washington, American Council on Education, 1940. 135 pp.

——— *et al., Thus Be Their Destiny.* Washington, American Council on Education, 1941. 96 pp.

Report of the Arguments of Counsel in Case of Prudence Crandall, Plaintiff in Error vs. State of Connecticut, Before the Supreme Court of Errors, in July 1834. Boston, Garrison & Knapp, 1834. Pamphlet.

Report of the Conference of College Religious Workers, Fisk University, Nashville, Tennessee, March 7–10, 1929. Pamphlet.

"Report on the National Conference on the Problems of the Negro and Negro Youth, January 6–8, 1937." Report mimeographed and available at the office of Mary M. Bethune, National Youth Administration. Washington, 1937.

Richardson, Leon B., *A Study of the Liberal College.* A Report to the President of Dartmouth College. Hanover, Dartmouth College, 1924. 282 pp.

RUGH, C. H., *et al.,* "The Essential Place of Religion in Education," *Moral Training in the Public Schools.* New York, Ginn & Co., 1907. 203 pp.

SCHLIPP, PAUL A., ed., *Higher Education Faces the Future.* New York, Horace Liveright, 1929. 269 pp.

SEARLES, HERBERT L., *State Constitutional and Legislative Provisions and Supreme Court Decisions Relating to Sectarian Religious Influence in Tax-Supported Universities, Colleges and Public Schools.* The National Council on Religion in Higher Education, Bulletin V. New York, 1924.

Second National Conference on the Problems of the Negro and Negro Youth. Proceedings. Washington, 1939.

SHEDD, CLARENCE P., *The Church Follows Its Students.* New Haven, Yale University Press, 1938. 327 pp.

———— *Two Centuries of Student Christian Movements.* New York, Association Press, 1934. 466 pp.

TEWKSBURY, DONALD W., *The Founding of the American Colleges and Universities Before the Civil War.* New York, Bureau of Publications, Teachers College, Columbia University, 1932. 254 pp.

THOMAS, GEORGE F., *Religion in an Age of Secularism.* Princeton, Princeton University, 1940. Pamphlet.

THWING, CHARLES F., *A History of Higher Education in America.* New York, D. Appleton & Co., 1906. 501 pp.

The Students Speak Out! A symposium from 22 colleges. New York, New Republic, 1929. 269 pp.

TOWNER, M. C., ed., *Religion in Higher Education.* Chicago, University of Chicago Press, 1931. 327 pp.

TUTTLE, H. S., *A Social Basis of Education.* New York, Thomas Y. Crowell Co., 1934. 574 pp.

———— *The Campus and Social Ideals.* New York, published by the author, 1936. 88 pp.

UPHAUS, WILLARD E., and HIPPS, W. TEAGUE, *Undergraduate Courses in Religion at Denominational and Independent Colleges and Universities of America.* The National Council on Religion in Higher Education, Bulletin VI. New York, 1924. 94 pp.

VIETH, P. H., *Objectives in Religious Education.* New York, Harper & Bros., 1930. 331 pp.

WARNER, W. LLOYD, JUNKER, B. H., and ADAMS, WALTER A., *Color and Human Nature: Negro Personality Development in a Northern City.* Washington, American Council on Education, 1941. 301 pp.

WEIGLE, L. A., *et al.*, *Religious Education.* Volume II of the Reports of the Jerusalem Meeting of the International Missionary Council, New York, International Missionary Council, 1928. 71 pp.

WHITEHEAD, A. N. *The Aims of Education and Other Essays.* New York, Macmillan Co., 1929. 247 pp.

WICKENDEN, A. N., *Youth Looks at Religion.* New York. Harper & Bros., 1939. 212 pp.

WILKERSON, D. A., *Special Problems of Negro Education.* Washington, United States Government Printing Office, 1939. 171 pp.

WILKINS, ERNEST N., *The Changing College.* Chicago, University of Chicago Press, 1927. 132 pp.

WILLS, E. V., *The Growth of American Higher Education.* New York, Dorrance & Co., 1936. 225 pp.

WOODSON, CARTER G., *The Education of the Negro Prior to 1861.* New York, G. P. Putnam's Sons, 1915. 336 pp.

——— *The Mis-Education of the Negro.* Washington, Associated Publishers, 1933. 198 pp.

——— *The Negro in Our History.* Washington, Associated Publishers, 1931. 673 pp.

WOOLMAN, JOHN, *The Journal of John Woolman.* Whittier edition. Boston, Houghton Mifflin Co., 1871. 315 pp.

WORK, MONROE N., *Negro Year Book, 1924–1925.* Tuskegee, Negro Year Book Publishing Co., 1925. 520 pp.

WRIGHT, RICHARD, *Native Son.* New York, Harper & Bros., 1940. 359 pp.

B. PERIODICALS

ADAMS, DAVID E., "The Study of Religion as an Integrating Discipline," *Journal of Bible and Religion,* 5, 28–30, January-February-March, 1937.

"Aims and Objectives of Church Related Colleges," *Christian Education,* 19, 26–36, October, 1935.

"Aims and Objectives of Church Related Colleges," *Christian Education, 19*, 311–317, April, 1936.

ANDERSON, RUTH E., "Why Teach the Bible and Religion?" *Christian Education, 14*, 33–40, October, 1930.

ARNOLD, S. C., "Education among the Freedmen," *Methodist Quarterly Review, 60*, 43–57, January, 1876.

ASPENWALL, LURA, "Status of Chapel Service in 48 Colleges," *Christian Education, 19*, 37–42, October, 1936.

BADGERS, HENRY G., "Finances of Negro Colleges," *Journal of Negro Education, 9*, 162–166, April, 1940.

BEILER, IRWIN R., "Some Implications of Our Teaching Aims," *Christian Education, 14*, 632–641, February, 1931.

BLANCH, L. E., and RUSSELL, JOHN DALE, "College Course Offerings in Bible and Religion," *Religious Education, 28*, 374–379, October, 1935.

BLANCHARD, E. Q., "Quarter Century in the American Missionary Association," *Journal of Negro Education, 6*, 152–156, April, 1937.

BLANTON, R. J., "The Future of Higher Education among Negroes," *Journal of Negro Education, 9*, 177–182, April, 1940.

BOWEN, J. W. E., "An Apology for the Higher Education of the Negro," *The Methodist Review, 79*, 723–742, September–October, 1897.

BRADEN, CHARLES S., "An Introductory Course in Religion," *Religious Education, 33*, 105–110, April–June, 1936.

BROOKS, BEATRICE ALLARD, "The Place of the Study of Religion in the Liberal Arts Curriculum in the Light of the Recent Theories of the Higher Learning," *Journal of Bible and Religion, 6*, 187–194, Fall, 1938.

CHIVERS, W. R., "Religion in Negro Colleges," *Journal of Negro Education, 9*, 5–12, January, 1940.

COE, GEORGE A., "What Makes a College Christian?" *Christian Education, 14*, 8–15, October, 1930.

CURRY, A. BRUCE, "Teaching the Bible for Life Values," *Christian Education, 14*, 642–645, February, 1941.

DANIEL, V. R., "What Are the Opportunities for Functional Citizenship in Colleges for Negro Youth?" *Quarterly Review of Higher Education among Negroes, 4*, 10–12, January, 1936.

DAVIS, A. P., "The Negro Professor," *The Crisis, 43*, 103–114, April, 1936.

DAVIS, JOHN W., "Report of the Committee of Findings of the Conference of Presidents of the Negro Land-Grant Colleges," *Quarterly Review of Higher Education among Negroes, 6*, 156–159, April, 1938.

DENNY, WALTER BELL, "Religious Services in the College," *Christian Education, 14*, 777–783, May–June, 1931.

DU BOIS, W. E. B., "Education and Work," *Journal of Negro Education, 1*, 60–74, April, 1932.

——— "The Field and Function of the Negro College," *Fisk News, 6*, 1 ff., June, 1933.

ELLS, WALTER CROSBY, "Survey of Lutheran and Methodist Colleges," *Christian Education, 19*, 133–143, December, 1935.

FOX, HENRY J., "Our Work at the South," *Methodist Quarterly Review, 58*, 29–44, January, 1874.

GILLIS, JAMES N., "The Church and State in Higher Education," *Christian Education, 19*, 170–175, February, 1936.

GRIMSHAW, IRVAN G., "Securing Teachers for Church Colleges," *Christian Education, 19*, 404–406, June, 1936.

HARKNESS, GEORGIA, "Teaching Content for a Philosophy of Religion," *Christian Education, 13*, 491–498, April, 1930.

HINER, FRANK P., "A Prerequisite for Teaching in a Church College," *Christian Education among Negroes, 21*, 92–97, December, 1937.

HOLMES, D. O. W., "Curriculum Offerings in Negro Colleges Contributing to Functional Citizenship," *Quarterly Review of Higher Education among Negroes, 4*, 1–9, January, 1936.

——— "The Role of the College in the Development of Character," *Quarterly Review of Higher Education among Negroes, 7*, 271–277, October, 1939.

JACKSON, REID, "A Democratic Philosophy for Negro Teacher-Education Institutions," *Quarterly Review of Higher Education among Negroes, 6*, 108–122, April, 1938.

JOHNSON, CHARLES S., "The Problems and Needs of the Negro Adolescent in View of His Minority Racial Status: A Critical Survey," *Journal of Negro Education, 9*, 344–353, January, 1940.

——— "The Social Setting of Negro Education," *Journal of Educational Sociology, 12*, 264–274, January, 1939.

JONES, D. D., "The Faculty Member as a Cultural Force in the Negro Liberal Arts College," *Quarterly Review of Higher Education among Negroes, 7*, 33–36, January, 1939.

KEPLER, THOMAS S., "Organization of the Courses in Religion," *Christian Education, 23*, 217–221, February, 1940.

KING, STANLEY, "College Chapel," *Christian Education, 19*, 277–281, April, 1936.

KOOS, L. V., and CRAWFORD, C. C., "College Aims Past and Present," *School and Society, 14*, 499–509, December 3, 1921.

LAMPE, M. WILLARD, "Facts and Impressions Concerning the Present

Status of Religion among Students." Association of American Colleges, Bulletin XXI, November, 1935. Pp. 458–461.

——— "The Place of Credit Courses in Religion in Tax-Supported Institutions," *Christian Education, 12,* 91–98, 1928.

LANIER, R. O., "Reorganization and Redirection of Negro Education in Terms of Articulation and Integration," *Journal of Negro Education, 5,* 369–374, July, 1936.

LAUBENSTEIN, PAUL F., "Developing Appreciation for Religion in the College," *Religious Education, 30,* 13–19, July, 1935; *36,* 234–344, October–December, 1941.

LEFTWICH, L. L., "Administration of Religion in the Liberal Arts College: A Theory of Religious Integration," *Religious Education, 36,* 234–244, October–December, 1941.

LORAM, CHARLES T., "New Opportunities for the Negro College," *Southern Workman, 63,* 168–176, June, 1934.

MAGERS, ROY V., "The Christian College and Citizenship," *Christian Education, 22,* 69–73, October, 1939.

MARKS, E. S., "The Negro College," *Journal of Educational Sociology, 12,* 288–297, January, 1939.

MATLOCK, L. C., "The Methodist Episcopal Church in the Southern States," *Methodist Quarterly Review, 54,* 103–126, January, 1872.

MAY, ROLLO R., "Portrait of Men Students," *Christian Education, 19,* 318–325, 394–402, April, June, 1936.

MAYS, BENJAMIN E., "The Religious Life and Needs of Negro College Students," *Journal of Negro Education, 9,* 332–343, July, 1940.

MCCUISTON, FRED, "Support of Public Education in the United States: With Special Reference to Negro Schools," *Journal of Educational Sociology, 12,* 257–263, January, 1939.

MELAND, BERNARD EUGENE, "The Study of Religion in a Liberal Arts College," *Journal of Bible and Religion, 5,* 62–69, April, May, June, 1937.

MILLER, KELLY, "Reorganization of Higher Education for Negroes in the Light of Changing Conditions," *Journal of Negro Education, 5,* 484–494, July, 1936.

MOORE, LLOYD V., "A College Program for the Teaching of Religion," *Christian Education, 21,* 83–91, December, 1937.

"Negro Health," *Time Magazine, 35,* No. 15, p. 41, April 8, 1940.

PADELFORD, FRANK W., "Twenty-five Years in the Colleges," *Christian Education, 19,* 210–218, February, 1936.

PANNOKOKE, C. H., "Some Necessary Changes in the Curriculum of the Church College," *Christian Education, 19,* 289–295, April, 1936.

PATTERSON, F. D., "The Aims of Negro Schools," *Occupations, 14,* 540–542, March, 1936.

PEARNE, THOMAS H., "The Freedmen," *Methodist Quarterly Review, 59,* 462–480, January, 1877.

PETERS, E. C., "The Curriculum of the Liberal Arts College and the Demands of a Bi-racial Society," *Quarterly Review of Higher Education among Negroes, 2,* 116–119, April, 1934.

PURINTON, CARL E., "Can Religion Be Taught Effectively in the Colleges?" *Christian Education, 15,* 53–62, October, 1930.

REYNOLDS, L. R., "The Curriculum of the Liberal Arts College for Negroes and the Demands of a Bi-racial Society," *Quarterly Review of Higher Education among Negroes, 2,* 102–108, April, 1934.

SCHWAB, PAUL J., "The Place of Biblical Instruction in Achieving the Objectives of the Department of Religion in College," *Christian Education, 22,* 55–62, October, 1936.

"Securing Teachers for Church Colleges," *Christian Education, 19,* 105–109, December, 1935.

SHAW, AVERY, "The Place of Religion in Higher Education," *Christian Education, 13,* 615–626, June, 1930.

SHEDD, C. P., "The University Pastorate," *Christian Education, 19,* 198–206, February, 1936.

——— "Religion in the Colleges," *Journal of Bible and Religion, 8,* 179–187, November, 1940.

SHERMAN, J. L., "Church-related Colleges Must Clarify Their Objectives," *Christian Education, 23,* 132–134, December, 1939.

SIMS, W. H., "Religious Education in Negro Colleges and Universities," *Journal of Negro History, 5,* 166–207, April, 1920.

SOUTHALL, EUGENE P., "The Attitude of the Methodist Church, South, toward the Negro from 1844 to 1870," *Journal of Negro History, 16,* 359–370, October, 1931.

SUMNER, FRANCIS G., "Philosophy of Negro Education," *Educational Review, 71,* 42–45, January, 1926.

TALLEY, M. A., "The Problem of Religion in Negro Colleges in Our Country," *The Sunday School Informer, 5,* 6–11, April, 1938.

VAN TUYL, MARY C. G., "Where Do Students 'Lose' Religion?" *Religious Education, 33,* 19–20, January, 1938.

WALSH, J. D., "Educational Work of the Methodist Episcopal Church in the South," *Methodist Review, 58,* 329–347, May, 1886.

WARNER, W. LLOYD, "American Caste and Class," *American Journal of Sociology, 62,* 234–237, September, 1936.

WEBER, LOUIS R., "Teaching Physics with Moral Objectives," *Christian Education, 20,* 350–354, June, 1937.

WEDEL, THEODORE O., "College Students and God," *Christian Education, 20,* 97–105, October, 1936.

WICKENDEN, A. C., "The Effect of the College Experience upon Students' Concept of God," *Journal of Religion, 12,* 242–267, April, 1932.

WICKEY, GOULD, "A National Survey of the Religious Preferences of Students in American Colleges and Universities, 1936–37," *Christian Education, 21,* 49–55, October, 1937.

WICKEY, GOULD, and ECKHART, RUTH A., "The National Survey of Courses in Bible and Religion," *Christian Education, 20,* 9–45, October, 1936.

WILKERSON, D. A., "A Determination of the Peculiar Problems of the Negro in American Society," *Journal of Negro Education, 5,* 324–350, July, 1936.

——— "American Caste and the Social Studies Curriculum," *Quarterly Review of Higher Education among Negroes, 5,* 67–74, April, 1937.

WILSON, W. W., "The Methodist Episcopal Church in Her Relations to the Negro in the South," *Methodist Review, 75,* 713–723, September, October, 1941.

C. REPORTS OF ECCLESIASTICAL BODIES

American Baptist Home Mission Society, Annual Reports, 1842–1890. New York.

American Missionary Association, Annual Reports, 1850–1890. New York.

ARNETT, B. M., ed., *The Budget,* containing annual reports of the General Officers of the African M. E. Church of the United States of America. Xenia, Ohio, Torchlight Printing Co., 1881.

Board of Freedmen's Missions of the United Presbyterian Church, *Our Work among the Freedmen.* Cincinnati, Ohio, 1911.

Freedmen's Aid Society of the Methodist Episcopal Church, Annual Reports, Cincinnati and Chicago, 1867–88.

Friends' Council on Education, *Two and a Half Centuries of Quaker Education.* Proceedings of Anniversary Meeting, Tenth Month 20, 1931, Philadelphia, Pennsylvania.

D. UNPUBLISHED GRADUATE DISSERTATIONS AND THESES

ARMSTRONG, B. K., "Factors in the Formulation of a Collegiate Program for Negroes," Ph.D. dissertation, University of Michigan, Ann Arbor, 1938.

JOHNSON, HENRY M., "The Methodist Episcopal Church and the Education of Southern Negroes, 1862–1900." Ph.D. dissertation, Yale University, New Haven, 1939.

KNOX, ELLIS O., "The Trend of Progress in the Light of New Educational Concepts in a Group of American Colleges Dominated by Religious Influences." Ph.D. dissertation, University of Southern California, Los Angeles, 1931.

SUMNER, F. H., "The Mental Health of White and Negro College Students." M.A. thesis, Howard University, Washington, 1932.

INDEX